#MeToo, circa 1927
The Quest for Meaning

by Mary K. Carr

Copyright © 2019 by Mary K. Carr

All rights reserved. No part of this publication may be reproduced, distributed, or transmitted in any form or by any means, including photocopying, recording, or other electronic or mechanical methods, without the prior written permission of the publisher, except in the case of brief quotations embodied in critical reviews and certain other noncommercial uses permitted by copyright law.

Front Cover: Photo taken by my brother Dr. John Davey (Jack) outside our family's summer cottage in Crescent Park, Canada.

Front Cover: Lotus is an Adobe stock photo.

Faust, Part One

*Until one is committed, there is hesitancy,
the chance to draw back,
always ineffectiveness.*

*Concerning acts of initiative (and creation)
There is one elementary truth
The ignorance of which kills countless ideas
And splendid plans:*

*That the moment one definitely commits oneself
Then Providence moves too.*

> *All sorts of things occur to help one
> That would never otherwise have occurred.*

*A whole stream of events issues from the decision,
Raiding in one's favor all manner*

*Of unforeseen incidents and meetings And material assistance
which no one could have dreamt would come their way.*

> *Whatever you can do, Or dream you can, begin it.
> Boldness has genius, power, and magic in it.
> Begin it now.*

-Goethe

Dedication

This book is dedicated to Marianne Wisbaum.

When I wanted to quit, she wouldn't let me, but she also got me back on track.

Acknowledgements

I would like to thank Sister DeSales Hattenberger who was willing to help and so very competent.

I also owe a very special thank you to Miss Alice Vale, the principal of Nardin Academy in Buffalo, New York, who played a major role in my childhood; she didn't give up on me. She considered me highly intelligent and saw that while I was not willing to study or do my homework, I was always respectful. Also, she recognized that I did not know enough on my own to mature, and she helped me. Because of her, I blossomed, was accepted, fit in, and acquired many friends.

Additional thanks to Dean Jacob Hyman, who so generously gave me Letters of Introduction when I decided to move to Washington. He was noted for several major accomplishments: the inauguration of the annual participating Fund for Legal Education, the successful celebration of the 75th anniversary, the revitalization of the Law Alumni Association and his support for state and local government studies.

As a teacher, he was cerebral rather than theatrical. One went to his classes to learn, not to be entertained. As an administrator, he deserves high praise. As a person, Dean Hyman scores the very highest. He left an indelible mark on countless students, a great role model of what it is to be a gentleman and a scholar.

Thank you also to Kathryn Radeff, without whom I would not have been able to resume working on this book.

Thanks to Linda Marie Franchell, who consulted with me on many issues.

Thomas Unger, PhD, who proved how much that sincerity counts.

Table of Contents

Dedication	4
Acknowledgements	5
Foreword	7
Preface	8
Introduction ♀ The Woman's Movement	9
Chapter One α Mary	13
Chapter Two ~ The War Years	31
Chapter Three ~ Law School	45
Chapter Four ♂ Harold	54
Chapter Five ~ Interim	67
Chapter Six ~ Political Appointments	71
Photo Album	77
Chapter Seven ~ Administrative Law Judge	89
Chapter Eight ♡ Bill	102
Chapter Nine ⚘ Mary	110
Chapter Ten ▢ Mother	117
Chapter Eleven ~ Uncle Jim & The Hanover's	122
Chapter Twelve ~ Siblings	125
Chapter Thirteen ~ Willie the Cat	126
Chapter Fourteen ~ Spiritual Journey	132
Chapter Fifteen ω Conclusion	145
Epilogue	148
Appendix I ◊ Diagnostic Study of a Personality	150
Appendix II ◊ Sri Lanka	157
Appendix III ◊ Lichtenstein Letters	162
Bibliography	166
About the Author	168

Foreword

"Mary, you are, what they call Mahatma in Hinduism. You are a great and very special soul. You have been served inadequately, but then you are so much beyond it makes that fact moot."

Nothing was ever too much for Mary to tackle. The greatest minds, but she tried to understand them and/or to be more accurate we tried together.

Mary was always open to all forms of thought and made every effort to understand many of the great minds such as Pier Valet, Dali Lama, or the many Christian contemplatives.

We met many interesting people on our journey and found great joy in the companionship.

Mary had the opportunity to spend time outside of the US hearing the Pope, going to Buddhist sights in Asia and learning an appreciation of such phenomena as chanting, and observing the many interesting places. There comes a time when the search subsides. Reading becomes more a matter of still loving to learn but enough has already been learned to have a more peaceful approach. At that point, there is gratification and appreciation, and the purpose of the journey becomes known as a wonderful life experience.

Mary and I met at a meditation group and there was instantaneous friendship. My background was in the teaching profession. My interest was primarily in Eastern Spirituality. I obtained a PHD with a dissertation in primal awareness. Additionally, I taught in various schools in Western New York and ended my career at Valencia College in Orlando, Florida.

Robert Hofteiser

Preface

Author Tracy Kidder said when you write the story of your life, you meet a new person. I did not know that, but I sensed it. After so many years of dedication to my spiritual journey, I had to become acquainted with the person who experienced it.

But my pen would not cooperate. It kept going back to day one. I learned that my spiritual journey started on the date of my baptism. Unfortunately, it took me a lifetime to be able to con- centrate on and devote my time to it exclusively. Oh my, what happy days were the results.

My spiritual journey had a framework. That is growing up, a career, marriage, and all other aspects that make for a life. Mine was at a time in history when my life reflected where society put women on the evolutionary scale, and more happened if they wanted other criteria. The suffragettes were gone and Betty Freidan, a leading figure in the women's movement in the US, had not yet arrived on the scene. So it seemed as though in keeping to yourself in many respects, one lonely trail was to be expected.

Introduction ♀ The Woman's Movement

I was sick. Nobody seemed to know what was wrong. I was in the hospital and was told that I would never again return to the world as I knew it. I was faced with an out-of-pocket bill of $500 per day.

Then I received the following poem, written by my six-year-old, very good friend, and it made me aware that love is all that matters. It made me smile and I fell fast asleep.

INDIGO

Indigo, Indigo is her name
Stealing my stuff is her game
She hits me, bites me
Pulls my hair
I tell my mom it isn't fair
She draws on my homework
And she goes all berzerk
But I wouldn't trade her
For a green alligator
She gives me a hug
If I give her a shrug
She snuggles with me at night
Even when I am a fright
We are sisters forever
Never to part
She will always be there
In my heart

—Isabella Fukushima

"I have yet to hear a man ask for advice on how to combine marriage and a career."
- Gloria Steinem

The women in my family did not wait for the suffragettes or give much thought to what was appropriate gender-wise.

They wanted to make money and did make money. They did not look to their husbands for permission or assistance. In the case of great Aunt Sarah, her husband learned early on, to both have her permission and obey. That was okay. He looked on his wife as extremely accomplished.

My father would always have been a believer in the equality of women and willing to in any way possible lend support. He was further interested in "what was the overall effect of giving women the right to vote." He was disappointed that their thinking seemed so close to the male of the species.

Through my father, I was always aware of such phenomena as areas of work that were predominantly populated by women being low paid. Further, if men became interested in such type of work, pay would improve.

Law was not of interest to me until the time I started to study it. Actually, I think I remember having a rather humorous attitude toward the fact that there would be 142 students in my law school class, five of whom would be "girls."

I was late taking a romantic interest in men, but certainly, that was mostly attributable to the fact that I had such low self- esteem with respect to both my looks and personality. It was about the time that I started in law school that I would hear remarks about taking up a man's seat and why didn't I get married?

The University of Buffalo graduated a woman from law school in 1897. Harvard admitted the first woman in 1951. Quite a contrast.

Upon matriculating in law school, the women who were practicing law were very few, but they were very strong in their feminine beliefs.

Mary Sickmon, who was singled out for respect among the women would make it a point to become acquainted with the "girls" entering law school. She would immediately admonish them to not think in terms of marriage but rather to leave that to women of limited intelligence. We thought she was bizarre. I thought of her as being a man hater. Then I saw her at the first Bar Association dinner I attended. She was sitting at a table with seven men. There was a bottle of whiskey planted in the center of the table and obviously, they were having a wonderful time. Mary Sickmon was a member of WCTU: Woman's Christian Temperance Union.

There were occasional incidents in an era when it was still appropriate for women to blush. It was not unusual for a legal case to involve a sexual question or obscenity. It was a question in the mind of the females as to how to handle this. Phyllis, a class-mate, always had boyfriends and seemed to get along well with men. I watched her. When the men laughed, she laughed. She really didn't call attention to herself.

One of the other women, Mary Ann, would always wheel her head around and look like she had no idea what was going on. One of the male students put a contraceptive on her chair as she was about to enter the room. She was horribly upset.

I dated a couple of the professors. It was an acceptable thing to do at that time. If I was not interested in a second or third date, it made things more difficult for me. When it came to my personal life at the time, my judgment was not that good. I wanted badly to go into a small law office and learn how to practice from the ground up. I tried at several offices but there was definite hesitancy to hire a woman. I had graduated 10th in my class and was an associate editor of the Law Journal. It was those facts plus my nerve, which landed me at the largest firm in Buffalo. I was very happy! At that time, it seemed like I was involved in reverse discrimination. The man in charge of placement said I would not have a chance.

My understanding was that my pay scale was half of that for the men and there was no question I would never advance to a partner.

My attitude toward this was that I would look at the positive. I was very fortunate to start my resume with such a good firm and I would stay under the pay circumstances only long enough to pay for loans I had incurred for school.

I did feel ambitious to have the experience of living outside of Buffalo. However, at that time, when staying at a hotel with my sister, unescorted women were not allowed in a bar after 5:00 pm. I protested when a waiter came over and informed us of that, I informed him, I was a guest in the hotel, but to no avail, I did not take it nicely, but I had to take it. I was being to get the picture.

I would have liked to be more of an activist in the women's movement, but I had a career manifested by persistently changing; always in different offices and cities and the result was not having sufficient roots.

With regards to the women movement, I did spend a period of time working for the Division of Human Rights. During this time, riots were occurring and I was in the midst of the fray. If one were to evaluate the suffering as the results of color dis- crimination and sex discrimination, my conclusion would be that in the final analysis, they are not comparable.

If for example a barber refused to cut a black person's hair the person discriminating would understand their license could be revoked and for exactly that reason. Disagree they might, but if they wanted to keep their license, they would stop the discrimination.

But with sex discrimination, no one understood why it was wrong.

Chapter One α Mary

"If you bring forth what is within you,
what you bring forth will save you.

If you do not bring forth what is within you,
what you do not bring forth will destroy you."
—Jesus, the Gnostic Gospels

On Candlemas Day, February 2nd, 1927, the dawn broke awash with overcast skies and an expected high of 28 degrees with snow. John and Nan made their way through the bone-chilling cold and piled gingerly into their car, a late model Hupmobile, at about mid-afternoon. Driving was an adventure and John could see his frosty breath as he bent down to crank-start the car from the front. The routine filled Nan with fear and foreboding as she would push the starter button and all the passengers would hold their breath until John could run around and jump into the driver's seat. Then, to the relief of everyone on board, they were able to begin threading their way through the icy streets of Buffalo, NY to their destination—Sisters Hospital.

    It was not easy for a very pregnant Nan to accomplish everything necessary between contractions but nevertheless, they made it safely to the hospital and at approximately 7:00 PM I emerged from the primordial soup. I was a small baby with naturally curly hair and given the name, "Mary."

    A week later, Father brought Mother and me home from the hospital. Waiting there for me were their older children, Ellen, aged three and one-year-old Jack, along with my father's mother, Grandma Davey and her brother, John Burns, known affectionately as Uncle Burns. Following my parent's marriage in 1923, Grandma Davey used her savings to buy a pair of two-family homes on Dupont Street in a working-class neighborhood on Buffalo's East Side. How Grandma was able to accumulate sufficient funds to purchase both homes was probably related to her thrift. I suppose my father had a quiet influence with respect to the chosen property. My mother, probably not, even though it was to be her home. My father was even able to persuade his conservative mother to vote for Eugene Debs for President on the Socialist Labor Party ticket.

The flat on Dupont Street was quite small, even though it had a living room, dining room, kitchen, and three bedrooms which were all quite small. It was the wrong neighborhood, the wrong neighbors, and the wrong structure of the house. It was not what Mother was accustomed to. She had been raised in a gracious, comfortable-sized home and selected furniture for her new home that was high-end and looked inappropriate in her new little house. Mother was not happy about living there.

The unsettling atmosphere was worsened by the difficulty of living with a strong-minded mother-in-law. For example, a day after I came home, Mother decided to give me my first bath. She came happily into the kitchen only to find that Grandma had risen early, forestalled her by bathing the baby, and was now starting to bake the week's supply of bread for the family. Mother fled to her bedroom, closed the door, and cried.

My mother was a former schoolteacher who had been compelled to resign upon her marriage to my father. At that time, married women were excluded by law from working as teachers. Both parents were of Irish descent. My mother was a short, plump woman with dark hair and blue eyes. Attractive and pleasant, she seemed to light up a room whenever she entered it. My father was fair-haired, good-looking, and even-tempered. Although he never finished high school, he was intent on becoming well "educated and had many intellectual interests, particularly economics.

Daddy owned a men's clothing store called "Gen's Men's Furnishing," on the corner of Oak and Genesee Streets. Initially, he had two other business partners but they dropped out soon after the store opened. He'd been a labor organizer before opening the first haberdashery in Buffalo to offer goods that proudly carried the union label. The store specialized in workingmen's clothing such as gloves, overalls, heavy wool jackets, and the like. My father would observe, albeit without bitterness, that the union members did not support his business, or feel loyalty to his cause.

A dark grim-looking place, it was the frequent haunt of various chums and associates of my father and included Bulgarians, Lithuanians, Poles, and other ethnic types who shared his interest in labor, politics, and the economy.

The business never really prospered; thus, it became necessary for Grandma and Uncle Burns to rent out their flat and move in with my parents and their children. It was at this time that the hub of the downtown area was surrounded by well-known businesses such as "Genesee Picture Frame" and countless popular taverns.

Originally, Grandma and Uncle Burns lived downstairs in one house. Uncle Burns was a quiet, gentlemanly man who had earned his living as a housepainter. At the time he lived with Grandma, he spent his days sitting at the end of the couch holding a corncob pipe to his mouth with a crooked arm and forever looking like Popeye the Sailor Man. He was always chief babysitter for the Davey children and would uncomplainingly and interminably get up and down as they would take turns shouting,

"I want a drink of water! I have to go to the toilet!" He died at age seventy, and to the consternation of Mother, was buried in a pine box like a pauper, because he had no life insurance or other monies.

Grandma's firstborn son, Joseph, and his wife, Elizabeth McNamara, a very pretty woman, lived upstairs in one house with their son, Frank. Another child, Eileen, burned to death at age six when her nightgown was set afire by candles as they were decorating the Christmas tree. Her mother was severely burned while trying to save her. The tragedy didn't end there as another daughter, Marion, died of a heart attack at the unthinkable age of eleven. Frank, a cousin and their surviving child, was a lifelong friend of the Davey family.

In the other house, my parents lived in the lower flat. The upstairs flat was occupied by the Johnsons, Walter and Cora, and their daughter, Marilyn. Also, in and out was Cora's sister, Jennie, who was suspected of being a "lady of the evening."

Cora sat most afternoons drinking beer at the kitchen table with the window open, talking to her neighbor across the alley who was also engaging in her afternoon libations.

Marilyn was an exceptionally pretty child with red curly hair, which was all lost as a result of an illness. She frequently hung out of the second story window by the fingers to the terror of her mother and anyone else who happened to see the little girl dangling from the side of the house.

Walter Johnson was never referred to by Cora by his name or in any other way but as "the goddamn Swede." We children wondered if she would go to hell for that. They were quiet upstairs except for holidays. They had beautiful singing voices and would join them together in a harmony that would begin early in the day. By the end of the afternoon and after much booze consumption, the picture would change. Fighting would commence and culminate by "the Swede" being thrown or pushed down the front stairs. Mother was appalled, Daddy amused, and the children mystified.

Grandma was a pretty woman, quiet and serene, but purposeful. Her parents were born in County Mayo, Ireland, often referred to as "County Mayo God help us." They came at the time of the potato famine on one of the so-called "coffin" ships.

They had five children. My great-grandmother, Mary Connery, died at age 33 and her husband, John Burns, at age 40. The tragic circumstances led to Grandma and her older sister being taken to a convent when their mother died. The nuns kept Grandma's sister and she became a nun, a professional teacher, and musician. However, like her father, she also died at the young age of 40. Grandmother was an attractive looking child so the nuns decided that she would marry. She began to work as a mother's helper at age ten and was self-supporting thereafter—a fact that my father bitterly resented.

When Grandma married at age 22, it was said that the prettiest woman in Buffalo married the homeliest man. When the grandchildren asked Grandma if she loved her husband, she would say, "He was alright, he was a good man." He, on the other hand, referred to her as a "wooden woman."

Grandma was intensely religious but in a private way. When I inquired about what she prayed for, her answer was, 'the grace of a happy death." She was a very passive woman, never contentious. One of her favorite sayings was "Suit yourself, and you'll suit me." The most negative remark I ever heard her make was "All you ever think about are your own four bones," leaving us grandchildren to wonder, which four? If the subject of happiness arose, Grandma would look thoughtful and say, "I have my work." She was considered a saint by all who knew her except perhaps by me. I realize now I blamed her for my mother's frequent absence.

My earliest recollections were of yearning for Mother, who spent most of her days at her Aunt Nan's house on Buffalo's West Side. I had naturally curly hair and Grandma liked to curl it, carefully forming each curl, while I seethed with resentment. Upon completion of the task, I would immediately shake out all her work. Grandma had suffered the death of two children from diphtheria at ages two and three respectively. Another daughter died of diabetes as a young woman just 24 years old, and a son of heart trouble at 28.

Her first-born, Joseph, was always a problem. Exceptionally bright, he was a silent person who was a truant from school, and later in life became a compulsive gambler who stole from my father and even pinched the Altar Society money from his own wife all to bet on the horses. He never actually supported his family so what they possessed came from Grandma. His wife left him and moved to California following the death of their daughter Marion. She had spent a year locked in her room after the funeral, and it was said that thereafter she never smiled. I loved her dearly and she would spoil me with baking powder biscuits. My first trip as a nineteen-year-old was to visit her in California. To the family's disbelief and consternation, Joseph followed Elizabeth to California and became a police officer.

One family story related how (as a boy), he'd had his long pants cut short after some unacceptable conduct; evidently, Grandma thought that childish behavior warranted a child's short pants, although she apparently felt herself responsible, at least in part, for his problems.

One Sunday morning, at a church on Grand Island, a priest gave a sermon about being a bad parent, and she had to be taken from the church in hysterics. It was unheard of for her to such emotion, and the family was mystified.

The one time I can recall Grandma Davey actually asserting herself in the child raising process was on an occasion when Ellen and I got into a fistfight and hair-pulling brawl. Ellen returned home late from a date, woke me from a sound sleep, and demanded that I move over to the cold side of the bed to accommodate her. I refused, and the battle was joined. As the imbroglio got louder, Grandma, who slept in an adjoining bedroom, calmly appeared in the freezing cold bedroom with a container of cold holy water and threw it over us exclaiming, "The saints preserve us!" My sister and I never fought like this!" Eventually, Mother arrived and mediated the skirmish.

For the most part, Grandma kept to herself and related only to my father, her much-loved son, John. He'd come home from the store after the family had finished dinner and eat in the kitchen. Grandma would sit at the table with him and that while he ate, read the paper, and half listened to her. They stayed close, and although she lived a whopping 85 years, Daddy was devastated by her death.

My paternal grandfather's father was an Englishman from Kent, who fathered 18 children. Little is known of his first marriage beyond the fact that his children had names like Hortense and Priscilla and were not raised in Buffalo. His second marriage was to Mary Manning who was born in Roscommon, Ireland. They had three children, including my grandfather, Joseph Patrick Davey, a painter who died in 1919. I did not know him or any of the Manning's.

However, the one story I do know concerning my grand- father is that he had atrocious table manners. At least, as the story goes, he had the common sense to advise the children to watch their mother eat. The Davey family inherited possession of a dagger received for valor by Patrick Manning in the Crimean War and a medal for valor received by another Manning in the Civil War. I think they were probably mercenaries.

The Irish settled in the First Ward, but my father's immediate family moved to an area located near downtown Buffalo known as the Hydraulics. It was also the area of Saint Patrick's, the best-known Irish church, where my father was active in the men's group. My mother disapproved of their kidding and their drinking.

My mother and her only sister, Mary, had been accepted for placement with the Grey Nuns at D'Youville when their mother died. The nuns did not make a practice of giving living quarters to orphans. They took the children as a favor to the Aunts. For the rest of her life, Mother wept when she saw a Grey Nun, remembering their kindness and nurturing. Several years later, her aunt Anna McNamara, (always called Aunt Nan), took them into her home where she and to a much lesser extent her sisters, raised them to adulthood.

My great grandparents on my mother's side, were born in Ireland around 1825 and emigrated to America on the Cunard Line at the beginning of the potato famine. Their tickets cost $12.50 per person. Upon telling this to my cousin's wife she immediately said, "They must have come steerage."

Honorah Morrisey, became aware of the opportunities that were available for women with an education in her new country. She took it upon herself, after birthing nine children, to open a business in the very tough area at the docks selling whiskey by the barrel. When her husband said he would never set foot in the business, she confidently said, "Don't, but my daughters will graduate from college."

Their daughters, Aunt Nan, Mary, and Bridget, never married; another, Sarah, married Alphonse Boutet and they adopted a child, Raymond. He was a hunchback. Both Raymond and his adoptive father were small men. By contrast, Sarah was a very large woman, with a demeanor to suit her size. They made quite a sight when they were all together. Raymond prospered eventually managing rat control for the city of Buffalo. On Sunday mornings, it was Alphonse's assignment to bring Sarah the New York Times while she remained in bed to read it.

During Prohibition, Sarah ran one of the distilleries of booze at Cozy Dell on the Niagara River in Canada. It was said that many Chinamen lost their lives crossing the River with their hooch.

"The Aunts," as they were referred to, founded the Reading Circle of Buffalo and were active in Buffalo literary and Catholic society. They sent their nieces to the School of Practice and then to Holy Angels, as both were considered as fine educational institutions. The aunts were high strung, given to constant dis- agreements, and forever bickered among themselves. They were kind to the two girls, and Aunt Nan was a constant presence and a steady, caring influence throughout their lives. The aunts continued to lavish care on their nieces, and "both graduated from college. Nevertheless, my mother always asserted that educational achievements were not as desirable as happy temperament.

I was baptized on March 6, 1927. Mother's close childhood friend, Helen Desmond Mahaney, and her mother's brother, Ted, stood as godparents, although neither played any role in my spiritual development. Aunt Nan who attended the baptismal ceremony studied my infant's face, and after some time commented (somewhat mysteriously), "She's deep as a draw-well." I've always felt her observation somehow presaged the deep interest I was to develop in the middle of life in the pursuit of spirituality.

On my second birthday, Mother decided it was time for me to graduate from a crib to a shared bed in the back room with Ellen. Ellen was a bed-wetter, but hopefully, that problem would soon be solved. When told of the plan, I became hysterical. I clung desperately to my crib, as it was taken away, screaming for help that did not materialize.

I've retained a painful remembrance of this traumatic incident throughout my life, although I later came to understand the dismay it must have caused Mother, and clearly remember the desperate expression on her face. I think the child psychologist, John Rosemund, would say that Mother handled the situation correctly. Yet I can still awaken the terror in my heart at being ripped from the warmth of that room off the kitchen with Grandma and Jack, only to be sent to the back of the house to share a bed with Ellen.

Though I adored her, she actually did not want much contact with me but instead, preferred a good book to my company. With Jack, I also yearned for his companionship but he too was decidedly aloof, a boy.

I felt terribly unprotected in that back bedroom and can still vividly recall waking up screaming convinced that someone was lurking in the closet. Trembling with fear, I watched as Father explored every possible hiding place, demonstrating that there were no boogiemen, goblins, or specters of evil waiting for the lights to go out again.

Frequently I awoke drenched because Ellen had wet the bed and Mother had to change the sheets. However, among all the challenges I had to surmount, none was as fearful as over- hearing my parents in the living room talking worriedly about the burden of paying their taxes and the ominous possibility that they might lose the house. I was terrified that we would have no place to live, and even though I had a bed to kneel beside for night-time prayers like the rest of the family, the comfort it provided was negligible at best—I was scared.

After Aunt Nan suffered heavy financial reverses in the stock market crash of 1929, her life became more circumscribed. In spite of the financial hardships, however, she did manage to retain two houses on Anderson Place as well as income property in the First Ward, which at that time was a mostly Irish enclave in South Buffalo. My mother used her aunt's home as a sanctuary from the constant, exasperating presence of Grandma Davey and Uncle Burns, and the stifling life she endured in the tiny house on Dupont Street. It was a refuge she sought almost daily.

Mother was further distressed by the sickness and death of her beloved sister, Mary, from heart failure in 1929. As little girls, Mother and her sister had faced the world essentially alone and had always maintained a loving interdependence. The aunts considered marriage undesirable for educated women and Mother had initially joined them in opposing her sister's marriage to a farmer from Eden Valley. However, when Mary insisted the marriage was important to her, Mother had supported her and the wedding went forward.

After her sister's death, Mother consulted the family physician admitting to him that she was hallucinating her sister was still alive. He responded by stressing her responsibility to her three young children. His counsel, along with Mother's strong faith in prayer, was able to help her recapture her perspective and stability.

Nevertheless, although she was a loving mother, she continued to suffer from bouts of depression throughout her life and as a result, was emotionally, and to a great extent, physically, absent through many of her children's formative years.

At around the same time, she confessed to her priest that she and my father had decided they could not afford to have more children, and consequently, was refused absolution. Thereafter, she attended Saint Michael's Catholic Church, served by Jesuits, and confessing the same decision, was able to receive the com- fort of absolution.

Following the stock market crash in 1929, Daddy, whose business had never been financially successful, became despondent and diagnosed himself as suffering from high blood pressure. Mother would have to outwit him to thwart his desires to leave with the family food money in the morning, leaving her with nothing to buy food for dinner. It was a nerve-wracking tug-of-war with their children's sense of security diminished as they helplessly watched the chaotic conflict. During the years that followed, money remained scarce and Daddy managed to stay in business supported only by the use of post-dated checks and his reputation for honesty—which enabled the store to struggle on despite a disproportionate debt-load.

I recall doing something or other that seemed very important at the time, for which I was promised a nickel. When the day came to receive it, my father said he couldn't give it to me but said he would be able to do so on a future day. When that day arrived, I renewed my request for the nickel. This time Daddy exploded . . . "NO!!" he bellowed. "You won't get it. It's your fault I don't have it, and you're nothing but a troublemaker!" His wild outburst left me totally devastated.

A short time later, Daddy took Jack and me with him to visit his friend, Mattie. Mattie was a character whose relationship with his niece (they lived together) raised many eyebrows. I accompanied Daddy into the yard alone without Jack, where Mattie gave me a nickel. I immediately thanked him and after some consideration, mentioned that my brother was in the car as well. To my delight, Mattie reluctantly handed over another nickel for Jack. After a little more reflection and in the realization that there was only one other, I boldly ventured to point out that I also had a sister at home. At that point, my father became exasperated with my persistence and angrily said he'd give me a nickel for Ellen when we got home.

As soon as we got into the car, however, Daddy ordered me to give Jack his nickel. Then he took the one Mattie had given me and gave it to Ellen as soon as we got home. Thus, as punishment for my forward behavior, I had to do without. This episode was echoed some thirty years later. As my mother lay dying, she gave me her engagement and wedding rings. My father angrily asserted that the rings belonged to him and demanded their return, whereupon he gave them to Ellen.

I desperately wanted Daddy's approval but was seldom able to earn it; a portent of my life thereafter. When he came home from the store, I'd often be listening to the radio and would try to persuade him to dance with me. He was a wonderful dancer and I remember how ecstatic and accomplished I'd feel on the rare occasions when he would pick me up in his arms and dance around the room.

He would occasionally play checkers with me, and I soon became pretty good. During one such game, I thought about each move, eventually catching my father in such a snare that in one more move, I was sure to win. Of course, I was delighted, but after studying the board, Daddy abruptly swept all the checkers away. I screamed at him, "You beat me, and I'm only a baby!!" He just laughed.

In the summer of 1932, Aunt Nan, as was her custom, rented a house for the summer. Tucked "into the picturesque panorama of Eden Valley, the entire Davey family, including Grandma and Uncle Burns, took up residence there for the season.

The rental, a big old white farmhouse, sat next to a beautiful brook that wound through the meadow like a silver ribbon. One of my earliest and fondest memories was me walking down to that creek as it flowed alongside the weathered farmhouse.

The house was only a couple of miles from where Mother's sister, Mary, lived with her husband who was a farmer. All the relatives, "shirttail" and otherwise, would automatically show up on Sunday for dinner. My father asked all the uninvited guests to donate a quarter towards milk for the children, but only once did he actually receive a contribution.

We children were allowed to play at whatever we wanted for hours on end without adult supervision or interference. The house had a tar roof, and one-day men were hired to re-tar it. As they gathered in the sunshine to eat their lunch, we three children hovered around their equipment, which included a bucket of hot tar. Somehow, Ellen and Jack convinced me that I'd enjoy being a tar baby, and as they poured the hot tacky tar over my head, my shrieks could be heard for miles. Despite fears that I'd be blinded, I survived the dreadful incident with minimal damage considering the potential for serious injury—a permanent bare spot atop my head—and even though I had suffered terribly at the hands of my older siblings, I continued to idolize both of them.

Looking back, I appreciate how wonderful it was to be able to play outside all day without my parents being fearful, but then— as now—there were predators. Along with the other children in the neighborhood, I visited the basement of a neighbor named Mister Grant, who was a skilled woodworker. He offered to make me a wooden box where I could keep my special belongings and jewelry. I was only alone with him once and on that occasion, he took me to a swing at the rear of his basement, stripped off my pants, and fondled me. I was completely confused by his conduct but curiously not afraid of him. Instead, I felt a confluence of feelings and actually had mixed emotions of part fear, and also an overriding sense of feelings of being uncomfortable and un- pleasant.

So, in fact, at the age of five, I knew I was being subject to conduct that was wrong. Thankfully, however, I heard my sister, Ellen, calling me and remember telling him I had to leave. Mister Grant hesitated but finally relented and gave me permission to leave. Ellen was calling me to take me to the church where she was going to confession!! I have always felt that this call to church may have saved my life—it certainly had a deeply meaningful impact on my future spiritual life.

The reality was that I wasn't old enough to participate in confession, but after making her promise not to tell, I did confide to Ellen what had happened. I later learned that she told our parents. Upon finding out that they knew what Mister Grant had done, I asked my father whether he was mad at him. His reply left me completely bewildered. "If I believed you, I would kill him," he exclaimed, and while his response confused me, I suspect he was trying to sidestep his parental responsibilities with respect to con- fronting a child molester.

The Grants moved away soon afterward, and the incident went unmentioned until some 60-years later. While visiting Jack and his wife, Joan, in Washington, Joan and I were in the car getting ready to go to play bridge when inexplicably Jack came running out of the house. He tore open the car door, sat down in the vehicle amidst our puzzled expressions, and out-of-the-blue after six long decades erupted with the completely unfathomable comment, "It took Mister Grant to put you in your place!" It was like it was something he had to do. He rushed out to do it before we drove away and then had a smug expression on his face.

What could have possibly prompted that remark from Jack after more than half a century had passed is an absolute mystery and was absolutely devastating at that moment sitting in the car with my sister-in-law. I did not even know that he was aware of the ugly incident from my childhood. Still, all curiosity aside, I believe that the destructive effects of that terrible event reverberated throughout my early childhood traumatizing me until I received psychological counseling in later life, which helped to heal me.

My second husband, Bill, always claimed that I was never really a child, and during the next few years, it seemed as though I went directly from the crib to the car keys. I have very few re- collections of those years and learned that memory loss is all too common among all victims of childhood molestation.

The event itself continued to be a dark, ugly secret, even from the men I was married to later in life. In retrospect, we, Davey children seldom played together. Once however, when we were home alone, we were playing at pushing and pulling when Ellen fell down and pretended, she was dead. Jack was terrified and it was evident that he adored Ellen in the same way as the rest of the household.

The few memories I can recall from that time include starting grade school in September of 1932. On the first day, Ellen walked me to my classroom. To my surprise and consternation, I wasn't to begin first grade, as expected, but to repeat kindergarten, which I attended the year before. As it turned out, Mother had agreed to do a favor for the teacher, who was a good friend, by placing me in kindergarten a year early so the teacher would have enough children to maintain a class.

Since none of this was explained to me, I thought I was being stigmatized as a slow learner and passionately resented the implication. I escaped from the school at the first opportunity and hid until it was time to go home. Of course, this upset all of the adults involved and they decided I needed to be watched more carefully. Despite the increased vigilance, I found an opportunity to escape again the very next day.

At that point, my parents and the school agreed to ad- minister an IQ test and, if the results were high enough, I would be allowed to start first grade. My score did pave the way for me to begin first grade, and I was overjoyed to no longer to be self- labeled a "dummy."

Along with a classmate, Milton Falkawitz, who had trouble pronouncing the letter "R," I was selected to announce the class play, an honor that I privately attributed to my baby lisp.

We were quite the combination. I thought the lisp was cute, and remained quite attached to it until high school, despite years of school- mandated speech therapy to eliminate it. My classmate and I were flattered by the reaction of amusement by the assembled crowd.

I earned passing grades throughout my elementary school years but little more, and in the fifth grade, I started falling asleep in class and was transferred to a "slow" class. I didn't stay there long. I must have succeeded in waking up—and while I had few companions—I do remember a friendship of sorts with my upstairs neighbor who was younger than I. My sister, Ellen, was an avid reader and always had a book open, while Jack was a typical rough-and-tumble boy.

My First Communion took place, and I was surprised and gratified to receive a beautiful white dress with smocking on it— the first I'd ever had that was not a hand-me-down. I filled my memory gaps by making up standard sins for confession: disobedience, lying, and so on . . . I found the whole subject of sin scary in one way and boring in another.

I was usually assigned the same penance: three Hail Mary's, three Our Father's, and an Act of Contrition. The latter prayer was one I continued to repeat for many years, especially when experiencing turbulence on an air- plane. I developed the practice of mumbling it hurriedly so that in the event of an "aircraft disaster, I would complete it before a potential crash.

Looking back on that time, I mourn the feisty child who was repeatedly involved in drama as the result of her determination not to be "done by." I had become a passive, obedient child with no behavior problems or troubles at school. I had, however, had a tonsillectomy and was frightened by seeing my parents and friends looking through a window at me in a hospital bed. I disliked living with so many relatives and longed for a nuclear family setting. I recall little more during age's six through ten than continuing to idolize my siblings while enduring sheer ambivalence towards our parents.

The dread of my life was my assignment to go to the A & P grocery store to buy basket-fired uncolored Japan tea. By today's standards, it would be considered fine dining, but to me, it was just one more example of what strange people we actually were. It capped the climax of Grandma's homemade bread when all of my friends had Wonder bread.

Around my tenth birthday, two things happened that shocked me. The first was a movie I saw at the Jefferson Theater, called "Things to Come." It was a scary British science fiction film in which the world regressed to a new dark age and it left me so terrified that I had continuous nightmares. I don't remember who accompanied me, but they were evidently unconcerned about ex- posing a very young child to such a frightening movie.

Maybe it was not that unusual that I was allowed to see that film or, better phrased, that my parents did not realize where I was or what I was doing at age ten. It was, however, the one incident that I was conscious of suffering so severely. Further- more, it strikes me to try and understand what were they thinking and the answer seems to be "nothing." They were not considering where I was or the effect that it would have on me.

The other traumatic event I endured was the Davey family's move to Aunt Nan's house on Anderson Place. The house was a large, single-family dwelling with five bedrooms, in a gracious middle-class neighborhood. It is now on the historic register; Aunt Nan owned the house and occupied the largest bed- room.

By this time Aunt Nan, as well as Grandpa Regan, had joined the household. The roster included Mother's brother, Frank,
who was devastated by his wife's leaving him. As a result, my parents had to give up their bedroom and sleep in the attic as did Jack who spent his teenage years with no privacy and no heat all winter—, which he accepted stoically.

I now had to ride my bicycle across the city to finish sixth grade at School 53. I brought my lunch and ate it at a friend's home, where I was given a glass of milk.

Mother said I should pay for the milk or bring my own, but I was too shy to introduce the subject and told Mother that they didn't want the money.

As it turned out, I was wrong about that.

One morning I fell off my bike and arrived at my friend's house a little bit late to find her in tears. She sobbed that her mother had said she was tired of supplying me with milk every day, that my own family could afford it far better than she, and I was not to go there anymore. In fact, our family was very poor during this period. We lived primarily on income from Aunt Nan and Grandma Davey's rental properties, and Mother despised having to deal with tenants. Daddy took very little responsibility for the family's finances although he continued to assert his status as a businessman.

When I was eleven, I became friends with a child from the upstairs flat next-door called Mary Anne. She had a pretty young mother with no visible means of support but many boyfriends. Also living next door were the house's owners and her son, who had a business renting hearses. The family was said to be connected to the Cosa Nostra. Although at the time, we were given to under- stand that Public Enemy Number One was living next door, and my family paid no attention to it. That suspicion had so little effect on their relationship with the Davey's that Jack was employed by them to "help haul stiffs." Almost twenty years later, the same neighbor turned up driving a limousine I'd hired for my wedding. I asked him why he hadn't brought his mother, and he said he hadn't thought of it. The pretty neighbor woman offered to take me, along with her daughter, to visit relatives in Pittsburgh. My friend and I, age eleven, excitedly went to Daddy's store to ask for permission to go. Mother was also at the store, and after asking many questions, my parents told us to wait outside for an answer. After a short, anxious wait, we learned the answer was "no." Furious, I decided to go anyway. I was afraid this might be my only opportunity to travel outside of Buffalo. I made Mary Anne promise not to report I'd been refused permission, and resolutely accompanied her and her unsuspecting mother to Pittsburgh. After several days, my friend's mother insisted that I call home. Of course, my angry parents insisted on talking to her, and she was just as angry when she learned of my deception. I wondered why there had to be such a fuss!

Usually, my family paid little attention to what I did, and I didn't feel that I'd done anything so very wrong. I was absent from school for several days, and when I returned, was directed to report to the principal. When she told me, she was undecided as to whether to let me return to school, I was bewildered about this continued flap. I assured her that since I'd already gone away, it wouldn't be necessary to repeat my absence, and there was no need for further discipline. I'm not sure she followed my reasoning. I was allowed to return to class. My punishment at home was a restriction to the backyard for several weeks. However, since no one showed any interest in my where-abouts, I quickly absolved myself from confinement and resumed going where I liked.

After the school closed where I attended the seventh grade, I was sent to the Cathedral School on Atlantic Avenue and Anderson Place, just down the street from my new home. The house on Anderson Place had no locks on the doors and became a gathering place for the teenage set.

On Sunday, I wandered into the kitchen and found my father listening to the events of Pearl Harbor on the radio. I felt quite excited at the prospect of there being a war and thought it would involve a lot of drama, which I would find interesting. I was curious at my parents' reactions of stunned horror and found the constant rumors of war somewhat boring.

Chapter Two ▢ The War Years

Work for peace in your heart and in the world.
Work for peace and I say again, "Never give up!"
No matter what is happening,
No matter what is going on around you, never give up.
—His Holiness, the Dalai Lama

September 1941 to June 1944

History would remember them as the war years—and so would I . . .

Initially, however, my world remained largely the same. Silly Nardin Academy periodically required its pupils to exit the classroom and lay down in the common hallway for air raid drills. It was always good for a loud giggle up and down the halls and a welcome break from the drudgery of schoolwork. The drills were a welcome distraction, but barely sparked even a scant interest in the fact that enemy submarines were offshore and waiting to get us.

As we made our way through these turbulent times and the historic changes they ushered in, I couldn't help but notice that the widespread burdens of the Second World War seemed to bring women an unprecedented immunity from their classically trained, gender-driven roles. Suddenly they were needed for more than cooking, cleaning, and child rearing. So, they hung up their aprons, rolled up their sleeves, and took on a man's world; they were shattering stereotypes. The nation's women effectively embraced traditionally masculine roles without compromising their femininity, succeeding in positions that reached from Rosie the Riveter, to the All-American Girls Professional Baseball League, to female factory workers, along with everything in between and beyond! The war was changing more than the geopolitical landscape. For in the midst of it all, the nation's mothers and housewives were becoming a defining moment rather than becoming defined by the moment.

Of course, like many families, it looked like the war effort was going to find its way into our home and that Jack would be drafted. Mother threatened to run away to Canada with him, and the mere mention of Jack's military service made Daddy's blood pressure soar. There was no patriotic claptrap echoing through our household. Daddy listened while Father Coughlin supported Hitler, as did Ambassador Joseph P. Kennedy. Okay, they may have just been spokespeople, but Daddy did not want them trying to use his son for gun fodder was my parental attitude.

On the day that I finished high school, there was the much-anticipated big external graduation event of my getting my diploma. The biggest event, however, was one to look forward to internally. It centered on other thoughts of meeting Mister Wonderful (who had been Tyrone Power but was now Howard Hughes). If only they would recognize what no other man had, namely that I was the most lovable female in the world, and—of course—after that, all of life's problems would be solved and I would bask in happiness eternally. Death was not part of my horizon.

At the beginning of my senior year, it did not look as though I would graduate. The only way around it was for me to finish a year of a history course in one term. With thoughts of keeping me back in kindergarten and putting me in a slow class in fifth grade echoing through my memory, I tore into that history book. Lo and behold, I found it very interesting and passed with flying colors.

That plus the fact that I made my own white eyelet piquet "princess style" graduation dress made me feel very important. My accessories included a dozen roses to carry and enough hair so that you could barely see my face.

Three distinct memories of my graduation remain. One, Lorraine Le Page, a fellow graduate, said she had been married that morning. I wondered what in the hell made her do that. Second, was the gift from my teacher, the book, "The Imitation of Christ," a Christian devotional by Thomas à Kempis. Thirdly, Miss Vale, the principal, said I had the distinction of being the most difficult pupil that she ever had.

Not that I was a discipline problem but that I could not be reached. She told this to Daddy and he took great joy in repeating it with laughter.

Well, I wrote all about my early years in some detail, so maybe telling what else happened to make Miss Vale describe me as she did can be elucidated by a brief chronological sketch of the years in between:

September 1939
I certainly did not fit in the last year in School # 30 so I may as well go to the one closest to home. It sure will be strange though going to a Catholic School.

September 10th, 1939
I really like this school, the Catholic School. I do wish I had learned to diagram a sentence before now, but if I strain, I think I can make it academically.

September 15th, 1939
Sister Winifred, our teacher, is very scary in her black habit with the white tunic. She seems very strict but she leaves me alone and I try to remain invisible. Don Kinsella, a good-looking showoff, was an altar boy at Mass this morning and mouthed off when he got back to school. Sister Winifred pulled his tie and he fainted.

October 1st, 1939
Most of the kids in my class have known one another for years and yet they are very accepting of me. I was made welcome in a social way that I had never experienced before. I wonder if it's because they are Catholics?

November 1st, 1939
My cousin, Jane Ellen, who is really pretty, and Don Kinsella are an item. It seems funny to have a cousin that I go to school with. She seems to be Miss Popularity snagging Don Kinsella while she's only in 6th grade, and they hold hands.

November 15th, 1939

Well, I decided to break the news to Daddy. He always comes home from the store long after the family has dinner and grandma follows him into the kitchen and talks to him in a desultory fashion while he reads the paper. After dinner, he comes into the living room and continues his reading. He doesn't usually put the paper down but he probably will in delight when I tell him my news.

So, I go headlong into it. "Daddy," I say, "I have decided that I will be a nun." No response, he just keeps reading the paper. "What do you think of that?" Just keeps on with the paper and says, "It might be alright." I remember he didn't even pronounce "alright" correctly. I don't think at the time I knew that his mother's only sister was a nun but I do know I was shocked by his response, which I considered very negative.

January 1st, 1940

I really have had an awful lot to be thankful for this year. I have four good friends, Alice, Mary Pat, Babe, and Jane Ellen, all my own age, and I really like Sister Winifred and the school.

Jane Ellen says our house is a boarding house because relatives live with us: Grandma (from the day I was born), Aunt Nan (so we could get away from Dupont Street with the garbage cans at either end of the block), Grandpa, his was a pronouncement which Mother felt she had to obey (there was also a financial incentive), and Uncle Frank (I think Mother truly felt compassion for him as the lame baby of the family). Uncle Burns had long since died.

Mother legally had to resign from teaching when she was married in 1922. Married women were not permitted to teach at that time. (I guess you might say the lives lived by her three children might be called dizzying when you think of the convent-bred young woman who had graduated from Teachers College and wed the labor organizer businessman who had not completed high school.)

So anyway, the gearing up for, and the war years were up- on us. Mother was called by the school department and asked to return to teaching. She was shocked and seemed to have no confidence but she was brave.

She would tackle anything to make a buck and so with nine people in the house to feed, back to work she went. Every day after school, she took her ration stamps and grocery money, shopped, and then got the dinner for nine people. We usually ate in the dining room except for when Jack was in the throes of a model airplane that could not be touched. Jack screamed and yelled his way into a vocational high school over Mother and Daddy's vigorous objections and spent the rest of his life criticizing them for allowing him to do so.

In the meantime, Ellen was very pretty and was followed by a deluge of boys and girls from Lafayette High School. Grand- pa listened to the radio and was especially fond of Peggy Curson, a beautiful young woman who played scales on the piano. When
last known, she had been admitted to the Psychiatric Center on an emergency basis.

Florence, the poor little rich girl, presented herself as Ellen's best friend. She did not easily attract the opposite sex but obviously increased her opportunities by engaging in activities with Ellen who had many different boyfriends. Florence danced to a recording, and Ellen at the same time read a book—all in the same double parlor and at the same time. The house on Anderson Place jumped with activity from the time Florence arrived in the morning to practice dancing before walking with Ellen to school, until late evening when Jack would walk Alice home.

Mother was a compassionate friend to all of the girls who would share all of their teenage angst with her—Daddy observed the scene, but strangely or otherwise, I am describing a different era because the house could be full of teenagers but activities were confined to music, dancing, and sharing secrets.

I was ten when Ellen started smoking and I could not resist imitating her. So, I would snitch a cigarette and go up to my room and open the window and smoke. I felt that I was doing something adult and extremely evil. Afterward, we taught Mother to smoke and all went through hell quitting.

June 1940
I graduated from the Cathedral School. I made friends, which would last a lifetime, and in the process attained some social confidence. Also, I learned about how some of my con- temporaries lived: Alice with little money and a family of nine children, Babe with older sisters and brothers who all doted on her, Mary Pat with a divorced mother who had a boyfriend, and Jane Ellen whose obsession with sex seemed to exist from 6th grade on. She bravely led a deeply tragic life, and after seven children, she murdered her husband by stabbing him. They both drank excessively and she was physically abused by him in the extreme.

September 1940
Well, I am back in the abyss in my freshman year at Lafayette High School. I try to stay well behind Ellen and Florence when I walk to school. It would be awful if anyone found out I was Ellen's sister at school because I am so strange. Furthermore, I have no friends and it is so hard to stay awake that I fall asleep in my classes. I don't even go into the cafeteria for lunch. There are
a few other strange kids who sit on benches and eat alone. I am one of them . . .
Something funny really happened to me one day. A boy came up to me and said he was in an art course and would I think of coming to his class one time to be a hand model. I thought it was awfully strange but I went. I don't remember any social inter- change in the whole year except that one.
I was desperate. I could not continue on another three years in this fashion. Then I thought of Alice. Father Lucid had gotten her into Nardin Academy so that she could attend a Catholic school. I went to him and told him I wanted desperately to attend a Catholic school and asked if he would help me. The next thing I knew I was announcing to my parents that I was going to Nardin Academy. As far as I was concerned, it was a *fait d'accompli* and it did not seem to occur to them to oppose me.

So first, my life was saved by Ellen going to confession, second by School # 30 closing and my going to the Cathedral School, and now by my acceptance at Nardin Academy. Evidently, being a Catholic can save your life without any dogma.

September 1941

Here I am at Nardin under Miss Vale's unobtrusive but vigilant tutelage. Well, except for that history course I am a poor student. I can always go to the top in reading and vocabulary but not as the result of any study. We had one lay teacher that I re- member. She was talking as a futurist about transplanting organs. I led her up the garden path until she agreed that you could com- pose a separate human being. Then I asked which part would be accompanied by the soul. So, seeing it was 1941, she wanted me expelled and when Miss Vale wouldn't, she failed me in the course. Miss Vale, however, obtained permission for me to take the exam at Lafayette High School and I passed.

The last Alumnae Tea I attended, in June 2006, there were only two women older than I was, one of whom graduated ahead of me. Nardin now excels academically and athletically but in my day, the only exercise we got was dancing. Ballroom dancing was the vogue but we were not allowed to touch each other. That was okay though because we preferred not to.

Outside of school, I started my working life by babysitting. I was always fearful of being alone in a big house but from the get- go, I saved my 50¢ an hour to buy cashmere sweaters and
Pendleton skirts. Before I was 14-years old, I got a job in the yard goods department at Sears & Roebuck. I had to lie about my age because I wasn't old enough to get working papers but the man who I expected to be the love of my life worked in the toy department so I was determined to keep the job. He never did pay any attention to me even when I wore a cashmere sweater and a white plaid skirt. My only result was being summoned to personnel. When asked if I knew why I was summoned I said, "Yes!" thinking my age had been discovered.

Fortunately, I said nothing further and was told in the future to comply with the dress code of dark clothing.

March 1943

Well, as I would not have said at the time, "The shit hit the fan." It was my way to periodically stay home from school with a made-up stomachache. I loved to spend hours in fantasizing love stories and no one paid any attention to me during the day. One day Mother became overwhelmed by my conduct and tried to force me to go to school. She did not succeed and I still remember her exhausted look as she left for work.

After that, I started skipping school rather than staying home, and instead, walked downtown to go to the movies. I would get as many of the other girls as I could by persuading them to come along. One day I was spectacularly successful and a majority of the class had been organized to go to the movies. Miss Vale did consider expelling me. She took me to her office and sat watching me while I took the standard IQ test. She apparently questioned the results from the test I took with the rest of the class. In any event, she told me I had the highest IQ in the school and if I continued to live my life this way, I was destined to lead a most unhappy life.

A decision was made that I was a bad influence on Alice and therefore our friendship should not continue. That is perhaps the only part of the decision that was faulty. Alice had a dozen other things on her mind besides studying, which caused her academic problems, and the friendship continues to this day with Alice still very active mentally. So, the end result was that I could not have a Regents diploma since I had not passed the required number of exams but I achieved a "house" diploma and left with gratitude

April 1944

It was such fun sitting on the front steps of the school at lunchtime thinking up naughty things to do and say. Miss Vale paraded up and down in front but there was an element of fear that she had some listening device but that only made thinking up things to do and say evermore exciting.

She never interfered with us until one day she called to me that she wanted to talk to me. I was astounded and scared to death. She said to me that I was a tall girl who looked older than my years. She said the baby way that I lisped was incongruous and sounded silly from someone of my size. Ever since I was selected to announce our class play with Milton Falkowitz in First Grade, I had been attached to my lisp.

To the best of my knowledge, I never lisped from that day forward. What eight years in speech class did not accomplish, Miss Vale did in five minutes. Besides, like me, she was about 5'8" and I truly thought that she would sound silly if she lisped.

The day I passed the New York State Bar Exam, I telephoned Miss Vale to credit her with being instrumental in my accomplishment. I was sad to learn that she had just died.

June 1944

Well, I don't know what to think about life now. Mother spoke of the possibility of my going to D'Youville but I told her that without a Regent's diploma I could not get in.

We were brought up strangely as far as religion is concerned. Grandma spent all day praying and her son took every opportunity to knock organized religion. When he was supposed to take the three of us to church, he took pleasure in taking us for a walk in the country telling us that brought us closer to the Divine.

It was only later in life that I learned one could participate in organized religion and still appreciate nature, but Mother seemed to get real pleasure from the Mass and told me the Catholic Church is wonderful in its adaptive ability, but having finished with Catholic school, I thought I might experience other churches.

At this time, I really had to worry about Jack. He was accepted in the Officer Training Program for the Air Corps but before he started, the program was closed and all the 18-year-olds were put in the infantry. He wrote terrified letters home when he was in basic training at Fort Benning, Georgia. He was scared to death of being bitten by a snake and was glad to come home on leave before being shipped overseas.

I have a picture of him sitting in Grandpa's chair in the second parlor playing his guitar and singing "Born to Lose," an imitation of Roy Acuff. I had an experience of sadness that still brings tears to my eyes; it was overwhelming to see my skinny blonde brother manifesting his depression with Country songs. He didn't cry then but he told of the sobbing of the teenage boys who went on the ship to Europe having been trained in a few weeks to kill the Germans. He had no knowledge of how he got there or the conditions that prevailed which brought him to where he was. At a mere 18- years, his life was so sad it was hard to experience any happiness knowing what lay ahead of him.

He was in active combat for only a brief time when he was injured all down one side. He told of the fact that the most generous act one soldier could do for another was to give him dry socks; the kind soldier that carried him from the front line removed his own socks and replaced my wonderful brother's wet socks with his dry ones.

Jack's injuries caused him to lose a kidney, his spleen, and there was shrapnel in his heart, lungs, and leg. He would have to spend the next two years in the hospital, first at Nancy in France, then in England before being shipped to Walter Reed Hospital.

Our house was buzzing with activity more than ever as the result of soldiers being stationed at the Consistory nearby. Ellen attracted them but she had so many boys and girls attracted to the activity at "The Davey's Home" that it was for all practical purposes impossible for anyone to get a one-on-one relationship.

I was well underage but I had no interest in alcohol so I really enjoyed going with the soldiers to dance at Frank & Teresa's Anchor Bar, the original home of chicken wings. I had never had a boyfriend and was invited to go only when there was no other girl available—or so I thought at the time—although I am not so sure now. I was one of a few really good fast dancers and I thought that saved me from being a wallflower.

In retrospect, I had a dedicated interest in clothes and saved all my money from working to buy a few expensive ones. I was 5-feet 8.5-inches tall with a slim figure and naturally curly hair. I considered myself completely unattractive so if a boy paid attention to me, I assumed that he had to be a blind jerk. My only romance remained in my fantasy world. Alice was working at Adam, Meldrum, & Anderson's and that seemed about as good an activity as any, so I got a job in the Handbag Department for $19 a week with take-home pay of $17.95. I paid Mother $10.00 and had the balance for clothes and the rest of my other needs. It was rather boring work, which was relieved by having a pretty friend, named Lois.

She and I were completely subordinate to the older more experienced clerks and didn't dare approach a customer while they were available. In exchange, we would be given an occasional sale. One of the clerks was married to a soldier and I used to feel very sorry for her because she looked so worried a lot of the time and would get upset if she didn't hear from him.

The upshot was that Lois—my pretty friend—and I were fired on Christmas Eve. Somehow, the Personnel Manager had a handle on the situation and we were re-hired the day after Christmas, but I remember sitting looking at the fire that Christmas Eve and for the first time really being conscious of the phenomenon of depression. I did not exactly know why but I did not want to return to Adam Meldrum's and didn't—however, Lois did.

Now I had to face looking for another job. I was, as always, intensely practical, so I did not want to go without money. Uncle Frank, who lived with us at the time, had a friend who had a friend in management at the Telephone Company. It never occurred to me that anyone would hire me because of any skills I had, but anyway I was hired at the Telephone Company.

I was scheduled to start work late one day and was home alone except for the old folks—which I considered alone—when the doorbell rang. To the best of my recollection, it was the mailman at the door and he gave me a package addressed to Mother and Daddy. We had no secrets at our house and so I opened it to discover that it contained the Purple Heart. I remember having a feeling that I did not have any framework to react to this news and I guess I did not go to work because I was home to observe the reaction.

Mother, like me, just seemed dazed by the news but she still had to take her ration stamps and go to Elmwood Avenue and shop for dinner. She met May Sheehan at the store and told her about Jack's Purple Heart. May—being forever the savvy Irish woman—advised her not to get upset and jokingly said that they give out Purple Hearts when they stumble digging a foxhole. Curiously enough, the Buffalo News mistakenly described that as the event that happened to Jack.

Mother came home and got the dinner and I told her cousins (the Quigley's), what happened. Mother left after dinner and went to them. John gave Mother a tumbler full of whiskey and Mother came home drunk and lay on the couch in the second parlor keening away.

When Daddy got home, Grandma showed him the Purple Heart and he threw it across the room. For days thereafter, Mother wrote letters to anyone she could think of to get information about Jack. It was slow coming and I now know it was not an exciting time but rather a horrendous one.

When Jack was returned to Walter Reed Hospital, he was at the amputee annex. Mother and Daddy had to stand on the train from Buffalo to Washington, the only trip I ever remember them taking. When they arrived to search for Jack, they were constantly questioned as to which body part he was missing. They didn't know that the answer was "none" but his health was profoundly affected as was his psyche. Jack spent about two years in hospitals.

Well, I got a raise working for the Telephone Company and started opening the mail. As in Catholic schools, I again seemed to fit in socially and so made lifelong friends.

Those who were capable in the mail-opening slot could hope to be promoted to Representatives. They first devised a test for representatives from a foursome of which I was one. The woman administering the test evaluated me as having a monotonous voice and so I failed the test. I was absolutely devastated and had a real sense of un- fairness, which I voiced, all over the place. I was given a job in the Public Office as "Greeter" which was similar to that of Receptionist.

I still had all the expensive clothes and there they mistakenly considered me "good looking."

Grandma was at home and making a bed while everyone except Ellen was at Mass. Ellen was not religious and while a teenager, she had decided that she didn't believe any dogma of the Catholic Church. Grandma was a recluse from her early- eighties and a priest from the Cathedral brought her communion. Anyway, in placing a blanket over the banister, she fell through the air and broke her neck. I have always been somewhat superstitious of how often the Catholic Church was involved in major incidents in my life. Two men, who were walking down the street, came to Ellen's aid and Grandma was hospitalized for about a week and died. While waiting for the ambulance Daddy paced up and down the living room snapping his fingers and then went daily to the hospital. I remember visiting her once but there was no communication.

Grandpa started peeing in the sink. We all were horrified but no one in the house had the nerve to say anything to him so I devised a scheme. Uncle Frank would say we were accusing him of it and he was being threatened with respect to his happy home. It worked but not long after that Grandpa said it was time for him to go to the Brother's of Mercy as he was becoming a chore for Mother. He left but died very shortly thereafter.

This was the time of the ending of the war and so the boy- friends came home and everyone went into one-on-one relation- ships from their own home.

We had the three funerals via caskets in the living room, flowers on the door (a funeral wreath) and much drinking in the kitchen together with my mother's brother harmonizing to all the Irish songs.

It was during this time that Ellen married. She had no wed- ding and was not married as a Catholic having previously decided that religion was not for her. The man she married, Don Reichert, was extremely handsome and had been very attractive to all the girls. I don't think I ever got to know him well, but he was always nice to me. My recollection was that he was not that nice to Ellen.

I remember him insisting she hitchhike home from Syracuse where he attended University because he wouldn't spend the money on bus fare—she was working full time.

It was, I think, what was called a "war marriage." Ellen had been the prettiest girl in the senior class in high school and always nominated for Beauty Queen in college, so the prettiest girl married the most handsome man but the relationship seemed to have no firm basis. He was very upset by the break-up and came to me for solace. I only thought of him in a brotherly fashion and when I told him that I acquired a boyfriend, I didn't see him again.

When she separated from Don, she went to New York City to live in Greenwich Village and try her luck at the theater. She had been considered very talented by the drama director at Buffalo State College and also at Syracuse University. For my part, I was absolutely dazzled by New York City and Greenwich Village with all the nuances of its artistic subculture, its unique menagerie of creative people, and life itself as a medium of artistic expression. It was like magic to me.

Chapter Three ~ Law School

I see my life beckoning to me,
my past has paved the way
and now I am free.
The time is now,
the time is right,
to leave the dark
and walk into the light.
I can do anything I want to,
I can be anything,
I choose it.
My life is a miracle
and I'm grateful for it all

—Karen Drucker

Suddenly I found myself face to face with a completely new phenomenon: living in a household with a nuclear family for the first time. Uncle Frank was the last to leave. He went to live with his girlfriend "Vi." He never did get a divorce as it was against the teaching of the Catholic Church.

Jack was home and grumbling over the fact that he had to take make-up classes to enter college as the result of having attended a vocational school. Home was an upper flat on Anderson Place and I really enjoyed living there in a way I never did before. All the teenage activity had receded except for Florence's nightly visit for a free meal while contributing a cake from the Goode Cake Shop. Jack worked as a short-order cook and waiter at the Goode and was going to school on the GI Bill. He hollered at Florence for wearing her boots in our house com- plaining that she would not do that in her own home. It came as a real shock to me that she would put up with the criticism and take off her boots. I never thought we were entitled to that much respect.

Now a lackluster sense of aimlessness entered the picture in my life, accompanied by an inevitable depression. Any male that I attracted I figured there was something wrong with. My girl- friends' suitors were back home from the war and I was lacking both in hobbies and motivation.

It was a time when I became acquainted with Mother and Father in a more meaningful way and I found that I not only enjoyed their company, but I really was benefiting in terms of a philosophy of life.

By this time, I had made a lateral move at the Telephone Company to the position of cashier. I must have repeated the phrase, "That's $3.45 out of $5.00," a couple hundred times a day. Mother always considered me slow moving so I studied each movement and became the fastest, most efficient cashier possible, but I was so bored that I tried to concentrate on Daddy's view that I had job security and would get a good pension.

Some radio program or newspaper article told about how the riddle of your life could be solved by a psychiatrist. I decided that it sounded more realistic than a fortuneteller so I thought I'd try it. I explained it to Mother and she tried to discourage me but finally took me to our family doctor. He diagnosed me as a person who had not "found myself" and said that if I went to a medical specialist, he would be most likely to fit me into his practice. It was only due to my relentless insistence that he gave me a referral.

I called and made an appointment with Doctor Matzinger who had his office in a beautiful house in an old neighborhood in Buffalo. He told me he thought I could benefit from some supportive counseling and mentioned that there was also the possibility of psychoanalysis but he did not think I needed that. The result was I started my monthly visits, which consisted of, checking my blood pressure, talk therapy, and then my paying him
$5.00 "for each visit. It did cut into my small income but I found it worthwhile.

He started me out with a battery of psychological tests, explaining that they indicated highly developed persuasive qualities and therefore I could think of a future in law or sales. I thought that was pretty funny until he suggested I go to night school and take college courses. I told him that was impossible with my background but to prove it, I applied to the Millard Fillmore College at the University of Buffalo.

To my surprise and consternation, anyone with a high school diploma from anywhere was permitted the opportunity to take college courses in the night school regardless of the quality of their grades. So, the next time I saw the doctor, I was a full-time student at night. It was a good thing that I had always made it a practice to save money because I now had tuition to pay and thankfully, had enough saved to cover it.

In a Saturday class about Economics, I met Bob—lo and behold, I had a boyfriend. It was a bumpy ride especially when a group of us went to see a show featuring transvestites and I didn't get it. Not long after that, I broke up with him for reasons I can't remember—I only know that I found the experience overwhelming. At the University, I completed sixty-four credit hours in one-and-a-half years, which actually was the equivalent of two-years of pre-law coursework. I achieved above a B+ average and earned one solid B and all A's on the remainder of my classes. I found that I now loved school and was blessed with the most important gift in my life—the love of learning, which has carried me through many murky-waters.

My routine found me working at the telephone company from 8:30 to 5:00 then taking the streetcar to the University to make my 6:00 PM class. I continued my classes all evening and left for home after my 10:00 PM class. Unlike today's physicians, the doctor gave me medication so I could study all night at exam time. During the exam phase of the semester, I would sleep one or two hours a night—the work and study schedule was almost overwhelming.

One night while I waited for the streetcar, a motorist stopped his car and beckoned to me. I recognized him from my economics class and he explained that he was going in my direction and would give me a ride home. During the course of the drive, he told me where he worked leading me to mention that a close friend was the secretary to the president at his place of employment. When we got near my home, he asked if I would stop so he could have a sandwich and a beer. I was a little bit reluctant but he seemed all right, so I agreed. We stopped without incident, and then he took me straight home.

Saturday night I was playing bridge with the secretary I had spoken to him about. She asked why he was driving me home adding that he lived in the opposite direction with his wife and kids. At that point, my radar lit up and I grew a little suspicious of his intentions. The next week he again offered to drive me home and I noted that he didn't live in my direction. He acted very insulted and said he needed to go downtown to his office after a day on the road and at school. I felt foolish and got in the car with him. When he asked me to stop for a sandwich I refused, at which point he said he would like to date me. I said, "I do not date married men." He pressed a gun in my ribs and asked if that would persuade me differently. "Yes," I said feeling very frightened and asked him to put the gun away. When we got to my house, I made no attempt to get out of the car. We sat talking for ten-to- fifteen minutes and then thankfully, he bid me goodnight.

I ran into the house and poured my heart out to Mother and Daddy but to my chagrin and horror, they took the unthinkable stance. In their very disturbing view that this fellow student who was very married, whose home—and wife—was completely in the opposite direction, and who was blatantly hitting on me, then jammed a loaded pistol into my ribs to force me into submission was probably just fooling around . . . They simply blew it off, cavalierly dismissing a crime out of hand as if it was completely meaningless.

I didn't let it go, however, and prevailed upon two men who were in another class I was attending who I knew worked in the courts. I explained the situation and asked them to find out if he had a pistol permit. They checked the records and discovered that he did, in fact, have a permit to carry that weapon. I don't think that I told Jack about it because I figured he would react the same way as Mother and Daddy, and I just didn't need disappointment piling on disappointment.

I was terrified of going back to the class as he sat directly across from me staring at me. I asked one of the other men in the class if he drove as far as Main and Hertel. He said that he would give me a ride. In the car, I explained why I had asked for the ride.

He was furious saying that I had no right to involve him in any way in what was my problem—*just the picture of gallantry*. I took the streetcar without incident for the rest of the semester but lived in fear of that man.

I asked Mother if I could quit work to go to Law School. She didn't say yes, but sort of ignored the question and then made remarks about the need for their income at this time of life. Then two things happened. Jack was practicing his incessant scales on the piano one day. He had money from working all his life and while he was in the service. I asked him if he would lend me enough money to get started in school. He thought about it for a long time and to my surprise and delight said "yes!" It was shaping up to be a long hard road, but it looked like I was on my way.
Then, Mother's friend and cousin, Jane Quigley, came to see her one evening and revealed that everyone was talking about the way I was being treated. Jane said that all our friends and relatives who had children paid for their education while I was expected to hold down a full-time job and go to school nights. After that, Mother and Daddy loaned me money and I was allowed to quit working full-time and attend Law School.

September 1949

Here I am in Law School . . . When I told Daddy, I was going to attend his response was simply, "Do you think anyone would ever hire you?" I didn't answer. In a way, you could say that Law School was a four-letter-word spelled: W-O-R-K! I did surveys, clerked in a Law Office, worked in the Libraries, and many other ways to make a buck. In the meantime, the most important part of my life at that time was academic. I was always in the top ten academically but secondarily I determined to date every boy in the class who wasn't married. These were watershed years for me because I had so much fun both studying law and allowing myself a type of high school boy craziness, which I had missed the first time around.

The number of women who were in the profession was so few that we got to know most of them while we were still in school but I did not think much in terms of unequal treatment.

I thought the Grand Dame of Women Lawyers was truly over the top when she categorically told women not to get married because we were too intelligent. Frankly, I thought she sounded like a woman who couldn't get a boyfriend, but such was not the case. She had a steady boyfriend who supplied her with enough chocolate to make her fat.

Once a year the Women Lawyers of Western New York would meet with the Women Lawyers of Toronto in a professional gathering that usually attracted between 20-to-30 people. Among our more memorable activities was our collective toasting of both the current President of the United States and the sitting Queen of England. I found the toasts somewhat curious and even amusing for an ensemble of lady lawyers. The ladies from Toronto were most conservative.

From there I made my way to New York City to stay with Ellen while I took the cram course for the Bar Exam. From the time Ellen moved there, I loved visiting her and the city so much that the mention of its name would light me right up! Light-years ahead when it came to fashion, an expedition to NYC wasn't just a trip—it was an event—and I would save whatever money I could to buy clothes in New York when I visited Ellen.

But that was not all . . . We would see wonderful plays, eat at fine restaurants, visit swanky hotels, and delight in people- watching. Mitch Miller, the world-famous oboist had a radio show with a buffet supper, which we attended Sunday nights, and I really felt like it was larger than life. It was the Big Apple and just being in it made you feel like you were in the "BIG-TIME" . . .

July 1951

My love life seemed like a non-event. My two main squeezes, Salvatore and Jack, were otherwise occupied. Every- body always thought Jack was in love with me—I didn't, I think I fascinated him and he's the only man I would say that about, but I wanted all the dates I could get and he seemed to act like that was an affront to him. At the same time, I have to say I could always count on him.

I got everywhere I wanted to go while he was in the picture but I never felt that he cared about me in the way I wanted to be cared about. Then he got another girlfriend— the one he married . . .

Cappy was different. He had a girlfriend at his home in Utica, NY, when he started law school so we just went out as friends, but he always seemed to really care for me although he had the girlfriend back home. His father was a first-generation Italian who achieved success as a lawyer *and he selected the girl Cappy was going to marry.*

I was sad when Cappy came back engaged in our junior year, and I thought he was sad too. Though I would not date anyone engaged, we were in one another's company a fair amount. He confided to me that he did not want to be a lawyer but rather a history professor at Dartmouth where he did his under- graduate work. I think that Cappy felt that such a life also appealed to me.

At the end of the year, we were finally alone one evening and he asked me if I would be serious about him if he didn't marry. I did not really know the answer and so told him I wouldn't discuss it while he was engaged. He went home and I was told by our mutual friend from his hometown that he had gone alone to the Adirondacks for a couple of weeks and everyone felt upset about his intention, but he did come home and marry the girl.

I was clerking in a law office full time and met my first boyfriend, Bob, who was in a rental cottage with several men at Crescent Beach near our cottage. I suspect that from the time he laid eyes on me he thought, "This time she doesn't get away." I learned what the word "seduced" means. He worked on me slow- and-steady, not once getting concerned about my objections to going a step further, but always patiently pursuing the next advance. "Bingo," he finally succeeded and I remember saying, "Is that all there is?" to which he winced.

I soon learned that I had fallen into repetitive conduct and it never occurred to me to put limits on it—but lo and behold—I was late with my period, then there was some sort of altercation with Bob; I drove right over to his home to confront him.

We reconciled, but by another week, I was scared to death that I was pregnant. I never forgot Bob's reaction. He did not believe me that I was a virgin. This was overwhelmingly horrible to me, but then he added, "A stiff prick had no conscience." He said his mother had told him so he knew it was true.

By this time, I was looking rather sick and Mother insisted one night on knowing what was wrong with me. Jack and his wife, Joan, were staying with us for the summer and Joan was mighty pregnant. I finally yelled at Mother that I thought I was pregnant at which point she slipped into a raging case of vapors. Her "symptoms" included a half-hearted fainting spell, followed by yelling and screaming hysterically that she had been a good woman so what did she do to deserve this curse upon her.

My father observed Mother for a period and then said, "Did it ever occur to you that Mary is the one with the problem?" The evening ended like a funeral dirge with everyone silently going to bed; *the next morning I awakened saved*. Joan came into the bedroom and was the first to know. I still picture her with her big belly, jumping up and down with glee. No one gave me any advice, although, Jack made the observation that the conduct would not stop as long as I continued to see Bob. It was like a shocking cold glass of water that was absolute truth and I never saw Bob again. He went to Daddy's store one day to talk to him. Daddy told me of his visit but he never volunteered what Bob said nor did I ask him. I somehow felt pity for Bob. He was in pre-med when I met him originally and had goofed off and was no longer on track. I knew I was strong enough to support him to get him back on track. There certainly was a caring that may have been mainly sex but that's often a good start to a relationship. In other words, I thought I really had a lot to offer him and he blew it and I never looked back or gave a damn what he decided to do with his life. I was very quiet and emotionally numb for a long time after that.

Happily, I graduated from Law School and passed the Bar the first time I sat for it. Still, I was really nostalgic for that school. In addition to every man in the school I could chase, I had dated two of the professors.

On a scale of one to ten, they did not rate in my life situation. It turned out that one of them was in charge of placement, a little detail that scared the hell out of me. When I went to see him, he simply told me to go and ring doorbells.

I dreaded doing it but had no alternative. So, I started at one end of Main Street and worked my way down, from the Liberty Bank Building to the Marine Trust Company. The first office I entered was "Falk, Twelvetrees." I told the receptionist I had just graduated from law school and I wanted to talk to someone about a position. She spoke to Mister Twelvetrees on the intercom and he bellowed back loud and clear enough so that I could hear it, **"Tell her we don't want women!"** I thanked the receptionist and went to the next office. There was no law against discrimination in 1952.

The last office I went to was the Kenefick office, which was the largest in Buffalo at the time. A partner happened to be walking past the receptionist's desk and heard me inquire about a position. He walked over to speak to me, assuring me that he would speak to the hiring partner about interviewing me. It was more than lip service and the hiring partner seemed to like my credentials. I had had experience with real estate law in one of my clerkships and he said that he would speak to his partners and get back to me. I then reported to my professor who told me that I would not be considered at the Kenefick office since they would not hire off of the street, and then only from the Ivy Leagues. It seems that my professor got some bad information because the next day I got a telephone call from Mister Kenefick and was hired!

I thoroughly enjoyed working in the legal world and with the lawyers who were associates of mine. However, I never lost sight of the fact that there was a substantial pay disparity and a woman would never be made a partner. Furthermore, in spite of the lovely treatment on the surface, incidents occurred which demonstrated that one was not simply a lawyer, but a female lawyer. The hallmark of admission to the Bar was having your name put on the door to the office. Since a lawyer who was hired ahead of me failed the Bar twice, my name could not be up until he passed the Bar and was listed ahead of me.

Chapter Four ⚥ Harold

You must learn one thing.
The world was made to be free in.
Give up all the other worlds
Except the one to which you belong.
Sometimes it takes darkness and the sweet
Confinement of your aloneness
To learn
Anything or anyone
That does not bring you alive
Is too small for you.
    —David Whyte
    "The House of Belonging

June 1955, Washington, D.C.
Emotionally, it was like I was returning to the frightened, lonely person I had been as I blindly groped through my uneven teenage years . . .

I loved spending time with Jack and Joan but aside from that, my life was truly miserable. I went to live with three other women: one negotiated loans for the World Bank, another was a lawyer for the I.R.S. whose boyfriend was the ambassador from Ecuador, and the last was an administrative assistant to a congressman. They were simply too high-powered for me, and so I was glad when my political clearance was not forthcoming forcing my return to Buffalo where the Dean of the Law School, sent for me.

Dean Hyman gave me a letter of introduction to persons of substance in Washington and also to a lawyer who would steer me around. The day after I returned to Washington I was seated in the office of the Secretary of the Army, Governor Wilber Brucker. He assured me a place could be found for me in the Defense Department. Then I became assistant counsel in the Office of General Counsel for the Department of the Navy.

I was told that the Bureau of the Navy was going through a process called "empire building" which demanded warm bodies on the payroll even though there was no work for them.

When I started, I worked on a leftover action concerning a Liberty Ship but then for all practical purposes, I had no responsibility.

Because of the hiring, they ran out of office space and I was assigned a desk in the secretarial pool. I became so upset that I was physically sick and was totally unyielding about the fact that I would never occupy that desk. The counsel in charge of the bureau had not been the person who hired me and I think in his hindsight he became scared of what connections I might have; he assigned the desk to a male lawyer who came after me. My successor was apoplectic with rage and spent every day there- after looking for a new job.

I missed Mother and Father so much it hurt, besides missing everything about Buffalo. I went to our cottage in Canada for a vacation and decided to have a cocktail party for the associates in the old law firm. I telephoned one of the men I had dated and he told me he was engaged so I told him to come and bring his fiancée.

I had dated Harold, a doctor, for a couple of years before I left Buffalo but infrequently. A client at the law firm was selling her house but the property was zoned Residence 1 which meant that the purchaser, Harold, could not see patients there. Since he was a physician at the steel company in Lackawanna and he sometimes saw emergency patients at home at night, he needed the property rezoned.

I argued before the City Council in favor of a rezoning. To prepare my case I had to have, or pretended I had to have, his entire history—so he looked good to me. After the argument, one of the political henchmen for a Council member approached me about dating his boss and I pulled the line I always used when I didn't want to go out with anyone. "He's married, isn't he?" I said.

The henchman sort of backed-off but I ran right back to the office and told the partner whose department I was in. At first, he did not know what I was talking about but when he got it, he was furious. He said, "No lawyer for this office has to engage in that type of conduct to win a case." I wondered how many had been asked.

Harold's father had come down to City Hall to hear the oral argument and suggested to Harold that upon winning he should take me out to dinner. He would call me for a date occasionally but didn't seem much interested when I said I was leaving Buffalo.

Back to my cocktail party: I thought I had nothing to lose, so I called Harold and invited him. He accepted with enthusiasm, and told me afterward he didn't think I was interested in him. I spent the rest of my vacation with him and thereafter time in writing and phone calls. Then came a letter in which he asked me to marry him.

I was delighted by his proposal. I called Mother to tell her and got silence at the other end of the line. Finally, she said, "I don't know, but I hope it's right for you." Her voice sounded like she was in a pit. Both Mother and Daddy wanted me to marry Jack who was my law school boyfriend. As I see that picture, I was able to believe he was infatuated with me but with a love/hate dynamic. He wanted to feel neglected by all of my boyfriends but really never wanted to be committed to me. I had several proposals but he was not among them. Nevertheless, I would have to acknowledge that he was wholesome, stable, and all those good things. I danced with him at a class reunion after my divorce and he said I deserved better. I think he meant himself.

Mother's reaction to my news was startling. Harold told me thereafter how pleased my parents should have been to have their daughter marry an established doctor. Those were not my parents' values but they were closer to mine. In retrospect, I thought it was the best of all possible worlds. I was getting away from a job I hated. I still was terribly lonesome for Buffalo and I would have a beautiful wedding and move into a beautiful home.

How I felt about Harold: Whether I truly loved him when I accepted his proposal might be somewhat open to question but that I loved him when he was my husband is not. I truly loved Harold, and he me, but it was he more than I who quietly deter- mined that we could not live together, or to quote him, he said, "it would ruin my life."

In May, he met me in Washington with an engagement ring and we drove home to arrange an August wedding.

August 4th or 5th, 1955

I spent the summer preparing for my wedding. Mother had wanted me to be married in the tiny church in Canada and have a catered reception at the cottage. I wanted—and got—a fancy wedding in Buffalo at Blessed Sacrament Chapel with brunch at the Park Lane. Mother's would have been charming.

I remember being very busy that summer with Harold and I having no particular disagreements. A couple of days before the wedding I went for a ride with Mother and asked her if she thought I should go through with it. She grew very still as she thought— and thought deeply—until she finally admitted she simply did not know. Afterward, I found out that Harold never went to bed the night before the wedding but wandered through the house wondering whether to show up.

It was a beautiful summer day and everything went smoothly. We flew to New York City and stayed at a small hotel that Harold frequented. They knew him by name. The marriage was not consummated that night for which Harold apologized profusely and I wondered what he was carrying on about since we had the rest of our lives. Our honeymoon was strange. Our picture is still in the picture gallery of the Elbow Beach resort in Bermuda. We had lots of sex, good food, swimming, and more, but I was overwhelmed and kept falling asleep inappropriately. Harold would and could remove himself entirely from me while being in the same room. The night we took a boat ride with no quarrel or disagreement; he never spoke.

We sailed to New York on a boat I think called the Queen of Bermuda and when we got to our stateroom, Harold said he was going to get our dinner seating. I started to come with him and he said, "I wish I could leave you in Bermuda and don't follow me all over the ship." I started to sob and did so it seemed for hours. Harold came back to the stateroom and was totally in- different to my plight. I don't think we ever talked about it.

We sat at the ship doctor's table with another couple also assigned to it. They were newlyweds also and the wife never came to a meal.

Her husband said she slept on deck. I remember thinking we are not as bad as they. Harold was interested in art, literature, music, architecture, etc., and was very knowledgeable and unpretentious with respect to his expertise. He had a farm that he loved and was talented at gardening, raising crops, and it seemed to me about every ability known to man.

There was an exception and it was a big one. He could not relate to any other human being with ease or pleasure. He said he didn't think it was possible for anyone to have the number of friends I had.

It seems odd now but I promised him I would not work after our marriage but devote myself to having a family. Well, I never got pregnant. Obviously, I didn't have enough to do. I wanted to foster or adopt children but Harold said he would not raise the results of somebody else's screw. He loved and bonded easily with pets so I wonder if he wouldn't have done the same if I convinced him to foster. I think he was bitterly disappointed that I didn't become pregnant. He even made up an ectopic pregnancy I did not have. I went to an OB/GYN specialist and the doctor said that I should be able to have children and Harold should be tested. This sent Harold into a rage that lasted for days.

Harold talked in a string of profanities, which I used, back at him for the first time in my life. I hated vulgar language then as I hate it now. It seems to be so dark.

I spent a lot of my time that first year redecorating our house. Our cleaning woman was horrified at the manual labor I undertook but I enjoyed it. Harold wanted to dictate what I did and so announced that I should be able to function without a cleaning woman. I informed him that it was strange to me that all my life there was cleaning help in the household and now that I married a successful doctor for the first time, I had to do it. I challenged him to wash the reception room floor, which was quite large. He did it and it left him exhausted—*which ended that argument.*

September 1956 to August 1959

When I first started to write about my marriage to Harold, I did not think I would have much to say, but now I would say *it is a hard subject.*

I found throughout my life that I didn't enjoy the lack of responsibility, and Harold had odd living habits. He did not like regularity. He might prefer dinner in the middle of the night and a small glass of wine in the morning, but he did not drink the rest of the day.

I have to acknowledge he seemed to try to warn me before we were married. One day at his house in the afternoon, he was boiling a needle. My era had no exposure to drugs and either that or denial resulted in my not heeding his warning, but night after night he'd get on a subject (usually about another person that I knew), then rant-and-rave all night. If I was asleep, he would awaken me to listen to his raving and keep waking me up.

When my brother, Jack, had surgery, I went to visit him in Washington. This was without Harold's permission so the next thing I knew I had a letter from a matrimonial attorney suggesting that I might like to start divorce proceedings. At the time, infidelity was the only grounds for divorce so I wondered what he was talking about.

Once I returned to Buffalo, I went to stay with Mother and Daddy at the beach. I also went to see Harold's attorney and told him with a great deal of anger that there were no grounds for divorce. Then I went to see one of my classmates.

Several weeks had passed at this point but my classmate suggested that I had disadvantaged myself considerably by leaving the marital abode and why I didn't just return. Harold's father had been waiting in the wings and moved in with Harold when I moved out. The house we lived in was large in terms of that time with six bedrooms, servants' quarters, a fruit cellar, a wine cellar, etc.

So, home I went to dear Mother and told her of my plan. She looked very frightened. (Jack described Harold years later as having anger always fomenting just below the surface of his expression). Mother drove me to our house and I used my key to get in. My big problem was the bathroom. Only the master bedroom had an attached bath, but I have always had a phenomenal bladder so I thought I could wait quite a while and so entered the guest room. Fortunately, all the doors had keys.

I felt scared to death when I heard Harold's father enter the house and telephone Harold to tell him I was there. First came his sister, Marie, ranting-and-raving that I had no business in his house. Then I heard Harold come home and launch into an in- discriminate conversation with his father. No one addressed me directly. It was evening when I finally had to go to the bathroom. No one bothered me so I went to sleep and the rest is history. In spite of our ups and downs and difficulties, we got through the first year.

I went to Harold's travel agent and she suggested a trip on a ship, which was a converted Liberty Ship. It was now a ship that carried the mail as well as government personnel who were required to travel on American Bottoms. The trip was a matter of months but after much musings about it, Harold decided it was a good idea. We sailed from New York and put into port at several points along the Mediterranean, with Alexandria, Egypt being the final stop. It was possible to get off and travel overland for several days to a week at a time so we were able to see a lot of each country. There were approximately twenty-five cruise passengers and we sat at the ship's doctor's table and we had a very pleasant time socially.

  Ellen came to the ship when we departed from New York and Harold had one of his spells of raving all night the first night out. This time he was on the subject of my sister-in-law Joan whom he had only met a couple of times. I remember saying to him, "Here you are in the middle of the Atlantic Ocean thoroughly disturbed by someone you have no interaction with and who does not give you a thought." Curiously, for the rest of the trip Harold never had any other spells, was a joy to be with, and communicated with everyone. I wondered if it was the responsibility, he feels in his work that causes his disturbance.

  Our crossing was like glass until the second to the last day. Then suddenly everything was falling off the dressers. The clothes were falling down, and I looked over at Harold. There he sat in his life jacket and I asked him what he expected to do about me if the ship went down. I told him I expected everyone would be in the upstairs lounge praying so we should join them.

It turned out we were the only passengers walking around. We grabbed breakfast as it flew by and just wallowed in fear.

I thoroughly enjoyed Spain, France, Italy, and Greece, but the Middle East was where we were fascinated. I bought rugs, and brass tables and material, and just totally enjoyed the scary, romantic atmosphere in Lebanon, Jordan, Syria, and Egypt. In Jordan, we were told not to leave our hotel alone but I did anyway. I saw the headscarves, and the black eyes, and the bayonets over the walls, and ran in panic back to the hotel.

The ship's doctor was a bachelor who had given some thought to marrying. We spent some time with him and it was interesting to see the contrast when the three of us went to the bullfight in Spain. Harold watched with total fascination while the ship's doctor got sick to his stomach. I just turned my head when something was hard to watch.

The Middle East was, of course, teeming with problems even then but we seemed to take little interest. We sat with an Arab who was the manager of our hotel in Jordan while he described the plight of the Arabs, and we saw them wandering homeless. It seemed we knew very little about a vast and complex problem. We arrived back in New York to start the second year.

August 4th, 1957

I'm back in my beautiful home, I have come to realize that I fulfilled Miss Vale's admonition and became a professional woman, married to a wealthy doctor. It seems as though the only need I have for the perfect life is to become pregnant, but life does not go on that way. Harold continued to be most compatible for a while. Then he got terribly worried that he didn't treat me right, that he was not good enough for me. He became despondent over it and took to bed. All his patients had to be canceled and I finally (with his father's permission) called one of his classmates who was also a physician. He revealed that Harold's mother had suffered from mental illness and that as a medical student, he had to cut her down when she committed suicide by hanging herself in the basement.

Harold's classmate expressed horror at the drugs Harold used and referred him to a psychiatrist. The psychiatrist saw me and told me that Harold was extremely suicidal but he would still like to take the risk of treating him as an outpatient if I thought I could handle it. I agreed although I had some reservation, and thereafter the doctor said Harold insisted on transferring all his assets, including his house, to my name alone. I considered it an aberration and agreed but transferred them all back when we separated.

Harold gradually got better but unfortunately; the hostility returned. I don't remember much about our life prior to our separation but the events leading to the separation stand out in my mind. At Christmas time, he would not allow any company and we didn't even eat a dinner—I was struck by the horror of it. By contrast, the first year we were married, I had a family dinner in which I outdid myself to make festive.

At some point, he threatened me but I knew it couldn't be a habit as I wouldn't tolerate it. I suggested to him that the two of us make appointments with psychiatrists to see if we could get any insight into our problems. He made appointments with two doctors at Strong Memorial Hospital in Rochester since he felt that consulting someone in Buffalo might have an adverse impact on his practice. Each of us was to be interviewed separately.

After my interview, I saw the doctor who interviewed Harold. His words may have been blunt but they cut like a scalpel.

"Get away from him, he's dangerous." "I can handle him," I said. "No, you can't," the doctor replied.

Looking back on it, I would guess that the statement was exactly what Harold intended him to say. I was advised to separate and return to practicing law but I remember thinking I was too much of an emotional wreck to return to work.

Harold threatened my life a second time sitting at the kitchen table. I decided very dispassionately to demonstrate what the implications of his threat would be. As was his habit, he went to bed mid-afternoon to rest after surgery.

When he did, I telephoned the police and asked them to simply inform him of what would happen if I got a warrant for his arrest.

One officer was sympathetic; the other was not, but they went upstairs, knocked on the bedroom door, and told Harold they wanted to talk to him. He answered by saying I was lying and crazy, but they said that might well be but this is what would happen if what I said was true.

I locked myself in the master bedroom with the attached bath. He went up and down the stairs over and over all night. In the morning when it was quiet, I came out and he was gone. Marie, his secretary, called later in the morning to say he neither arrived at the office nor did he call. Harold had disappeared.

We had a family friend who was a private detective. He said he'd probably reappear spontaneously. He didn't. After a week, the detective came to the house where Mother and Daddy were with me to support me. He said after this length of time he was probably dead but to go through the attic and cellar to make sure he was not in the house. Daddy and I searched the house from top to bottom, the creepiest thing I ever did in my life. Upon completing our quest for Harold's remains, Harold walked in the front door.

May 1959
I asked Harold if he expected to go on with our marriage. "Yes," he simply said. "I can't," I replied. He took a trip to California for a couple of weeks and I climbed down off of it. I vacillated at times but never really changed my attitude after Harold returned. He had spent the week he was gone in New York City. He vacillated also but said quite thoughtfully one day that he was ruining my life and it would continue that way if we stayed together so he was willing to dis- solve the marriage for my sake alone.

I moved temporarily to the Park Lane. I was only able to get a room but it was large so I furnished it as a living room with a pullout bed and it was quite pretty. Harold insisted that I take all items of value that I could possibly use. He also wanted to buy me a new car and generally do much more for me than I was willing to accept.

Daddy talked to me when we were separating. He thought-fully advised me not to take support from Harold. At the time, it would have been quite easy to obtain it but in any event, Harold was quite willing to provide it.

"If you don't have to work you may not and your life would be wasted so be self-sufficient and use your education to support yourself," he said.

I returned Harold's assets and agreed to take periodic payments of $100 per week to re-establish myself. I still had some savings from before I was married and some from working a short time while I was married. When I found a permanent apartment at 800 West Ferry Street, I didn't think I could afford, it but Mother just said it's a good spot so go "make the money to afford it. They had more confidence in me than I had in myself.

Between May of 1959 and August, Harold and I were never apart. We got along as perfectly as we had on the cruise. Finally, my attorney called me into his office and said the lawyers could not go into court with the way we were acting. It would look like a fraud on the court.

So, with extreme sadness, Harold arranged a trip to Europe and one night we had dinner together. I had said I could care for our dogs while he was gone. He pulled into the driveway of the house and I said I could walk the block back to my apartment. I then told him I had reconsidered and would not take the dogs so I would say, "Good night." I never saw Harold again in my life.

August 5th, 1959

Supreme Court in the County of Erie Judge Matthew Jason presiding: My marriage was annulled and my attorney drove me home. I went to the beach. It was such a shocking experience. My parents and I took a long walk and I could talk but I felt over-whelmed by sadness. My memories are of the fact that we each wanted to try so hard to make a life together but it was impossible. Harold could not meet my needs nor I his, but curiously enough, there was a trust between us—or so I thought.

I was at the beach one day and reading a book while Mother was sweeping the floor.

She said to me, "Mary, there is something I would like to ask you if it's not too personal." I re- member being astounded by her formality and saying, "You can ask me anything you damn well please."

"Did you know Harold had been previously married," she asked. I pounced on her to say, "What silly talk was that, and where did you get such a peculiar notion?"

She said she had been in the optical store run by Harold's best man and he had asked for us. Mother had replied, "We had broken up." He then volunteered, "That was Harold's second marriage to fail."

I had dinner with Mary Ann Killeen a few nights later. She drove and as I was getting out of the car at the Park Lane, I turned toward her as if on an afterthought and said, "You knew of Harold's previous marriage, didn't you?" (Talk about entrapment.) She said, "Yes." I got back into the car and asked for an explanation.

She said one of our fellow associates, Charley, whose grandfather or great-grandfather was the presidential candidate who used the expression, "Rum, Romanism, and Rebellion," had been a patient of Harold's, and Harold had talked about his first wife to Charley. As a result, when my engagement picture appeared in the paper, Charley said to the associates, at coffee, "How come you Catholics can go around getting married all the time?"
One of my colleagues and a former classmate spoke up and asked him if he was there and commented that it would be admirable if he minded his own business.

I felt like everyone knew but me. I could understand why they didn't tell me, but at least they could go to the sacristy to notify the priest. So, no one spoke up to answer the ceremonial question about why Harold and I could not be joined in Holy Matrimony.

Fast forward 20 plus years: I'm sitting at the Marriage Tribunal and the priest telephones Harold and gets him on the first ring. He asked him to affirm a previous marriage. Harold told him, I was his wife, our separation had pained him mightily, and he would hear from his attorney in the morning. Never call him again. Six months later, he was killed in an automobile accident. I do understand staying in abusive relationships.

When it's good it is very, very good and you keep thinking this time the abusiveness will stop. I think I am lucky to have gotten out of it with my life—but I didn't—I got out without extreme emotional damage.

Chapter Five   Interim

*I am not afraid of storms,
for I am learning how to sail my ship.*
                              —Louisa May Alcott

September 1959

I didn't want to go back into law. Instead, I wanted to try social work and I wanted to work with children. It turned out that I went to work for the Children's Aid Society, which had a director with a national reputation. One of my first cases involved a seven- year-old girl who had been molested by her stepfather. He (the stepfather) and his mother told police that his wife was crazy when she reported it. His wife had been in and out of mental institutions so the police believed him and told the mother they would only arrest him if he was caught in the act.

Thereafter the mother called the police when a car happened to be in the neighborhood and he was caught in the act. However, that was not the most serious infringement—he made the mistake of socking the police officer. He was placed under arrest. The seven-year-old went to foster care, and a girl of five and a younger boy remained at home. We had a psychiatric consultation and were told that the man displayed the actions of an addict. If the seven-year-old were removed, but the younger children returned, he would just start in on the next in line.

I fought tooth and nail to have the three children removed from custody, but I got very little support. The agency worried about losing cases as a result of lawyers cross examination. Unfortunately, the mother had to be sent to the state mental institution. The outcome of the case was that the seven-year- old was retained in foster care and the two younger children were returned to the father.

Everyone at the agency was afraid to tell me, but I had fought as hard as I could, so the outcome was beyond my control. It was my duty to go to the mental hospital and tell the mother. She knew how hard I had tried and so she also was almost fatalistic about it. Thereafter, she was discharged and able to obtain custody of the seven-year-old. From there she took her to live with family in another state.

It was summer and Jack and Joan were going on an extensive trip to Mexico. Their daughter Katherine was about eight and their son John about five. Mother was quite worried about the fact that they wanted to leave the children with her. When I asked her, what worried her she said, "The responsibilities," and I said I was going to leave Children's Aid and would carry the responsibility.

I took the children with me to work and assignments I had. They both loved it. Then after I quit work we'd go to the beach or on an outing each day. Katherine was always a joy but at first, John posed a real problem. Finally, he threw a skate at me and I grabbed his arm and whacked him. He screamed and went to his room. There was general consternation with my mother yelling at me and John in hysterics. The next day he came and sat on my lap and we were friends forever after.

When Jack and Joan got home, they only stayed long enough to pick up the children who eagerly got into the car without saying goodbye. Mother was deeply hurt; I was bewildered.

After Harold and I broke up, I felt like an emotional wreck and decided it was time to figure out why I kept making moves that would make my life so difficult. I started in psychoanalysis with Doctor Heinz Lichtenstein. There were a whole series of situations and conditions that caused him to be willing to take me as a patient. I was very fortunate as I had been so often in my life when I needed help to find my way.

I didn't have to resituate myself immediately after my year at Children's Aid where I learned irrevocably, that I did not want to be a social worker. I decided I'd like to work on an indefinite basis rather than regular employment in an office that did general practice. I found the area of labor law rather interesting and knew a man who worked in a firm that did that kind of practice. He had been editor the Law Review when I was an associate editor.

In the latter office was Herald Fahringer, the noted defender of free speech! When my marriage to Harold Wass broke up, I fully expected to be done with love, but my relationship with Herald Fahringer was like a bombshell. I was terribly attracted to him and

I thought he was attracted to me as well.

The firm was willing to have me on a basis of being loosely associated and I started to do work for several of the partners. Gradually, however, I was spending all of my time doing criminal work with Herald. To me, Herald was handsome, bright and an excellent lawyer from whom I could learn a lot, but unfortunately, my hormones got in the way.

Herald had a girlfriend but would repeatedly ask me to have dinner with him. That was the period during which I was heavy into psychoanalysis and I always had to refuse him. I had no recollection of what incident or series of incidents caused our relationship to rupture, but I remember being miserable over it. At that time, I drank, which was an activity that always had a bad effect on me and I telephoned Herald after a martini. He came to my apartment immediately and we talked. He told me he had had strong feelings for me but that I always rejected his attempts to be with me. I told him I was in psychoanalysis and it appeared to scare the wits out of him. It was a long and intense conversation, but I think we both left it understanding there would be no further relationship. Harold made the big time in first amendment cases and with notable clients such as Claus Von Bulow.

When the Law Review had its 50th anniversary at the Buffalo Club, Harold was imported from New York City to be the main speaker. It was absolutely thrilling to me to talk to him and to have my picture taken with him. He was very pleased to hear I had been an Administrative Law Judge and wanted to know if I remarried. I told him I had and he said he thought I would marry
a lawyer. By this time in my life, I had stopped using alcohol and would have truly enjoyed having a reflective conversation with him. Of course, the opportunity didn't present itself, but I still enjoyed every second of the conversation and the picture taken with him.

I had started to become active politically as a Taft Republican and I passed a civil service exam and was appointed the supervisor of the Juvenile Legal Division of the new Family Court.

I had made up my mind that although Social Work per se was not my thing, I did want to work in the social field.
I set up the new Law Department and recruited Dorothy Murphy who had graduated from law school a year ahead of me and another lawyer together with two secretaries to help me. I found the work challenging and was surprised to find I really enjoyed being an administrator. I did a lot of work with the police and enjoyed training the police and sheriffs both alone and with one of the judges.

Chapter Six Political ~ Appointments

Carry Something Beautiful in Your Mind.
There are times when life seems little more than a matter of struggle and endurance; when difficulty and disappointment form a crust around the heart. Because it can be deeply hurt, the heart hardens. There are corners in every heart, which are utterly devoid of illusion, places where we know and remember the nature of devastation. Yet though the music of the heart may grow faint, there is in each of us an unprotected place that beauty can always reach out and touch. It was Blaise Pascal who said: In difficult times, you should always carry something beautiful in your heart.

—John O'Donohue in
Beauty: The Invisible Embrace

I met Norma at a political gathering and she told me her sister, Elayne, was looking for a travel companion to accompany her on a Caribbean cruise—, which I went on. When it was all behind me, one could conclude I was rather empty-headed seeking nothing but fun on that cruise. However, we had the good fortune of being seated at the Chief Engineers dining table and the officers as a group embraced us, using their entertainment allowances to arrange things we could enjoy.

The First Officer would rave about the woman seated with him who kept rubbing his leg under the table. He was incensed at her nerve. I'd laugh and ask him what he thought women went through all of their lives in the area of unwanted attention. He solved the problem by, as he described it, throwing her into the Staff Captain's cabin. The Staff Captain didn't partake in the entertainment and the story was that she stayed happily in his cabin for the rest of the voyage.

We got off the ship at Martinique and I was floating in the Caribbean when I had what I'd characterize as an epiphany. I felt totally and perfectly relaxed and safe floating in the Caribbean.

I experienced the perfection of pure unadulterated joy without any precipitating cause. It was a profound experience comparable only to my discovery of "The Imitation of Christ." Professionally I had become quite active in politics and got kicks when Senator Javits and Governor Rockefeller knew my name, but what a silly judgmental character I was then. I refused to have my picture taken with Margaretta "Happy" Rockefeller because she left her children.

While writing this, I can hardly believe I did that. Additionally, it was about this time that I was first listed in "Who's Who of American Women." The excerpt is as follows:

> Davey, Mary Katherine, lawyer;
> b. Buffalo; d. John Edmund and Anna (Regan) Davey;
> L.L.B., U. Buffalo, 1952.
> Admitted to N.Y. Bar, 1952;
> Associate Kenefick, Cook, Mitchell, Bass & Letchworth, Buffalo, 1952-55;
> Assistant counsel Office of General Counsel, Department of Navy, Washington, D.C.,1955-56;
> Supervisor Juvenile Legal Dept Family Court of Erie County N.Y. 1962-65;
> Case Analyst N.Y. State Commission for Human Rights, Buffalo, 1965-. Mem. Women's unit
> Executive Department State of N.Y., 1966-,
> Mem. Advisory Committee Cooperative Urban
> Extension Committee, Buffalo, 1967;
> Active various community charitable organizations.
> President Republican Civic Club, Buffalo, 1964-65;
> Board of Directors Federation Republican Women's Club, 1963-64.
> Mem. Women Lawyers Western N.Y. (president 1965-66),
> National Association Women Lawyers,
> Rep. Women Lawyers League (president 1963-65),
> Business and Professional Women's Club,
> League of Women Voters,
> University of Buffalo Alumni,
> University of Buffalo Law School
> Alumni, Nardin
> Alumni, Kappa Beta Pi.
> Home: 800 West Ferry Street, Buffalo 14222. Office: General Donovan Building, Main Street, Buffalo 14203.

I was Campaign Manager for John B Tutuska, a very popular sheriff and really learned what it means to run for public office. I found it stimulating, but exhausting.

Following Sheriff Tutuska's campaign, I had what was close to a collapse. I had ruptured ovarian cysts and a fibroid uterus. While I was in the hospital, the Clerk of the Court dismantled my department and subsumed it all under his jurisdiction. That, of course, would leave me with no job to return to. I could hardly believe it, but knew Dorothy Murphy would not lie to me. The only problem was all of these slots were in the Civil Service system. The day that I came back the Senior Judge told the Clerk of the Court that he could not prevail. So, everything went back to square one except I knew that the Clerk would go to any length to get my job.

Appointments had not been permanently made off of the Civil Service list and I—being one of the top three on the exam— was undeniably in the running. Judge Niemer, the senior judge, had shirt-tailed Tutuska all the way through the campaign and so was politically indebted to him. I had supported numerous causes so the local party was indebted to me. However, the Clerk of the Court prevailed in this situation. He convinced Judge Neimer not to give me the permanent appointment. He also had convinced him to go completely contrary to his own interests. Then word got out—*which it did immediately*. Tutuska, as well as the County Chairman, asked for explanations that Niemer did not have. It cost him the next election. The Clerk stayed just a clerk and never achieved his burning ambition to be a judge.

The Division of Human Rights had just been legislated into existence and the Commissioner was a political appointment. He was entitled to an attorney on his staff and I was recommended to him. So, I think it was within a couple of weeks that I found myself as Case Analyst for the Division of Human Rights.

In leaving Family Court, in addition to the work I loved, I was leaving two dear friends. Dorothy who had been with me from day one, and Mary Ann, Judge Niemer's secretary. Mary Ann was pretty and fun and she seemed to take a lot of the seriousness out of life.

We took a trip to Mexico together and had a high old good time. Mary Ann never believed in paying for her own dinner be- because she preferred restaurants that she could not afford. Consequently, she busied herself meeting whatever men were available whenever they were available.

Thus, we played and we really played . . . Out for half the night, touring during the day, and finding both the high life and interesting people in Mexico City, San Miguel De Allende, and Acapulco, etc. ... I was sick from the food for weeks after returning and loved all the weight I lost because of my illness. People thought we were very funny together as we bounced reparteé back and forth. She was also very active in politics so we continued in one another's company after I left the court.

June 1963

My career took me into a new world. I have had Black acquaintances through my life but that in no way prepares a person for total immersion into another culture. Suddenly I was living in a predominantly Black world both at work and outside of work for a good part of my social life.

I knew something was wrong, but I didn't know what. One day I went for a drink after work with the Regional Director who was Caucasian and Jewish. I remember sitting thinking and thinking, and finally asking with great vehemence what is wrong, what is the reason for the disparity? Victor Einach looked straight ahead and said dispassionately, "The color of their skin." It seemed to me no answer but it said it all.

I became close friends with an older black woman who worked with me. Since I was her friend, it was as though her family and friends were also my friends. She was also active in politics and if Mary Ann was my friend, she was also Alfreda's friend and so Mary Ann became "Miss Davey's baby sister." Mary Ann actually loved the whole gestalt of being accepted at Black functions and so we had another dimension of fun, fun, fun.

I again thoroughly enjoyed the work I did. I really was very fortunate since I seemed to move around so much to always land on my feet doing work I enjoyed.

It was at this time I started to go to New York City fairly often on business. I had gone once or twice while at the court and always loved it, but it was for meetings whereas with the Commission I had work to do. Another first was Bob Johnson from our New York City office. I had never had a Black man pay attention to me as a woman before and found it an intriguing experience.

One day he said to me, "Miss Davey, are you black?" (I am fair-skinned to a fault). "I don't know but I will ask my father," I replied. The next time I saw Daddy I told him of the exchange. He didn't answer me until a couple of days later. He said he had thought it over and he was sure I was not on his side but he wouldn't state positively with respect to my mother. Oh well . . .

Turmoil seemed to be my lot in life. After two years, the whole Division of Human Rights was to be reorganized. My Commissioner would be moved out and the word was that the job would go to a black person. To me, I could apply for it as well as other white persons and the job should go on ability, not color, but I had my sites on an appointment to the Appeal Board and was supported by some political backing. It proved not to be enough and so there I was, a white woman, a lawyer with some experience for hire.

I got what was a political appointment as Counsel to the Education Committee in the Assembly and now was in Albany three days a week. The abortion debate raged during this time and it was handled by the Education Committee.

My cousin Loretta came to visit me. She had been exhausted by having her daughter-in-law and grandchildren with her for a year and she said she just wanted to sit in a bubble bath for a couple of days. I took her with me in the morning and got permission from the appellant to have her watch a hearing. In the evening, I drove her down to watch a legislative proceeding. The bailiffs were removing women from the Assembly Chambers who purposely fell down, by pulling their hair and dragging them out under their arms. Loretta said, "Get me out of here." I said, "You don't understand Loretta, they are all Catholics." Her response was one word, "Out!"

    I had fun going to all of the functions the lobbyists hosted and it never occurred to me to make a judgment except that everything was free. I learned the expression, "Albany Wife" and also learned that many of the legislators were free, and so when Nelson Rockefeller was inaugurated, I was invited to the party.

They had a cadre of state police checking invitations. Mary Ann had come to Albany and blissfully danced past all of them and into the Assembly Chamber.

Photo Album

My paternal grandfather Davey with aunts and uncles, her father John, seated on the floor on right, and grandmother.

My nuclear family: Mother, Anna (Regan) Davey
Father, John Edmund Davey (holding Mary on his lap),
brother Jack, and sister Ellen. (1928 or 1929)

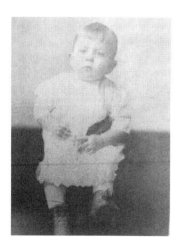

Mary K. Davey, age 1 – Already 'a force to be reckoned with!'

Cathedral School, 8th Grade Class Graduation (Me in the front row, with the bow, fifth from left)

Jack (third from left) and Ellen (2nd from right) with friends --during the war years

UB Law School Class of '52, one of only 5 women in the class (front row, 8th from left)

My engagement photo to Harold

Me, as a Bridesmaid on the stairs of the P ark Lane Restaurant in Buffalo

Wedding Photo: The bride (Mary Wass) seated next to her niece Katherine (flower girl – Mary's father John and first husband Harold are standing behind her to the left and right)

Bridal photo in a beautiful gown that I noted was inexpensive, especially given the quality

At a political dinner (seated on far right) during my political years

That's me, at the podium, teaching a room full of policemen a lesson in Family Court Practice

Photo from when I ran as a candidate for the NYS Constitutional Convention of 1967

Bill's 70th Birthday with his *very large immediate* family!

At the African Equator with Bill

Bill and me, Kenya, last trip at the Norfolk Hotel, Nairobi

Me and my "lost love," Herald at the
50th Anniversary of the Law Review

Law School Ladies

With my "soul mate," Bob

Fort Erie Spiritual Group

Brother John Meditation Group

Ellen Mary & Jack

The *"furry* love of my life" ... my cat Willie!

Jody, me & Mandy at my birthday party

Ellen's 90th Birthday

Chapter Seven ~ Administrative Law Judge

This is our purpose . . .
to make as meaningful as possible this life
that has been bestowed upon us,
to live in such a way that we may be proud of ourselves,
to act in such a way that some part of us lives on.
—Oswald Spengler

January 1970

    I have just completed a De Mello Retreat at Mount Carmel in Niagara Falls. An absolutely beautiful site with good accommodations and excellent meals, but for whatever reason (though I hate feeling like this), I felt somewhat out of place and self- conscious this week. It certainly is not that I can withdraw in my life. I attended one of these 20-years ago and I think that was about at the beginning of my spiritual journey but I will have more to say about that later.

    I interviewed in Albany prior to coming for an appointment as an Administrative Law Judge. I was quite skittish about actually moving from Buffalo because I was so lonely when I moved to Washington. It seemed patent that counsel wanted to hire me. He said my residence could be anywhere in the state if I just appeared ready to hold hearings on Monday morning. Judge Leonard Gelberg drove me to the airport and was told to talk up the job. I was so used to things being political I couldn't believe that I would be appointed on merit alone.

    However, within a short period, I got a telephone call offering me the job. I decided I would keep my residence in Buffalo and fly to Albany Monday mornings, which I was told was satisfactory. I was told I was the first woman to be appointed an Administrative Law Judge in New York State. Mary Ann drove down with me. I had cased the area so I knew
I could stay Monday through Fridays in the Tom Sawyer Motel located next door to the office and could leave my car in Buffalo.

I was only in Albany a few weeks when I was told of a woman (the cook at the Tom Sawyer) who liked to rent a room in her house to supplement her income—so by Monday, I was settled in. After the first week, I went on the road (in counties throughout New York State) with Murray as the judge and Barbara as the court reporter. I was terrified that Judge Murray would make me hold a hearing. When we got back to Albany Friday afternoon and Goldfeder found out that, I had not held any hearings he was furious and said he personally would take me to New York City next week.

On either the first or second hearing in New York City, I was listening to the New York City attorney asking for an adjournment to prepare for the third time. I said, "No" because he had no valid reasons. He looked absolutely shocked and when it was over, Goldfeder said in a meaningful way, "You know how to hold hearings." I kept my apartment in Buffalo for a year and liked being able to spend time with Mary Ann and the Hanover's as well as my father.

There was a very unfortunate estrangement from both my sister and brother and I don't even remember what the cause was. I do know it was involved with my psychoanalysis and seemed to be for the best all the way around. I don't remember how it came about, but seriously question whether it could have any salutary effect. Maybe there was some lack in self-sufficiency that was alleviated but in retrospect I can only say, I hope it was worthwhile for one or more of us, for whatever the reasons.

After that first year when I'd fly home, I stayed with Mary Ann. We had many fun-filled vacations together. While at the Division of Human Rights, Victor Einach introduced me to Chautauqua. Mary Ann and I would spend ten days there every summer. They were such happy days . . .

At work, I'd first travel upstate with a reporter for one week, spend one week in New York City, and then take one week to write decisions. I enjoyed the hearings so much. I also enjoyed traveling by the state-owned car to the counties all over New York. The reporters were all nice company and every once in a while, I'd be assigned with Barbara. It was a joy to have female company since all the other judges and reporters were male.

Originally, there were 12 judges who handled the state including New York City. We heard appeals from County Com- missioners with respect to public assistance, medical assistance, and originally aid to the elderly, blind, and disabled. We were one-week upstate, one-week NYC, and one week on decisions at the office. It encompassed the whole gamut of the human condition and I found it not only interesting work, but work that was satisfying in that you could truly change people's lives for the better.

We all had our lives threatened, as well as people threatening to commit suicide. One woman said her husband had put two old cars in her name. It was a result of his unwanted actions that she was cut off from public assistance. She matter-of-factly stated she shot him and if the action was repeated, she would simply kill him and put an end to the problem.

I had a case where a man who was dishonorably dis- charged from the military who was denied public assistance for neglecting to obtain employment before he left Vietnam. He stated that he didn't even own the clothes on his back and as a result decided to take them off. It was interesting to observe the consternation on the faces of the men in the room at the thought of his success.

We ate in a neighborhood restaurant run by a Jewish Mama. She'd take the orders from the men and then bring them what she thought was best that day. They would be frustrated but would not expose her. Lunch was paid for by going to the cashier and reciting what you had eaten. So much for cosmopolitan New York!

On one of our last weeks in Brooklyn, we had a state car and were leaving at Noon on Friday (breakaway day) to return to Albany. I was in the car with two male colleagues. After we had been driving about a half-hour, one man said his scarf was missing, the other said his hat was missing. I had taken a "doggy bag" from the restaurant we ate at the night before and it was missing. We discovered the state car had been broken into and the perpetrators got a hat, scarf, and lunch. I was the only one amused.

We were all friends—and more—close friends. When we got off the road, we would all meet at the Tom Sawyer on Friday afternoon for drinks to the consternation of all of the wives. Barbara (who lived with her twin sister), used to opine, "The men have their wives and I have Fran!" Fran was also unhappy when Barbara didn't arrive home.

I knew New York City in a different way. I worked there all week. Many of my colleagues were New Yorkers so they knew all the restaurants. When we had offices in the World Trade Center, we would walk back to midtown noshing as we went stopping in Little Italy, Greenwich Village, etc., and I thoroughly loved it. On weekends many of my friends from Buffalo would come down and spend the weekend with me and I would not return at all to Albany. I could pack in a flash and have everything I needed with me. It was an art, which I might add from experience, was lost when it was not practiced.

There would be tales to be told every week, which were high drama from New York City. One of the Judges in New York City was a friend of Al Pacino's and would often get a part in his movies if they were shot in New York. One day he told me that his first love was to be an actor, but after that, being an Administrative Law Judge in Social Services in New York City ran a close second for drama alone.

With time, we happened to fall into patterns. Bill, Paul, and I handled the New York City office, located in Brooklyn, quite regularly. We were known as "The Mod Squad."

We thereafter moved to the World Trade Center and with it, were given still another view of an experience in New York. The PATH trains, disgorging people in all directions, the uniqueness of moving all those people in a way that anyone can find their direction.

Flash forward decades... I don't turn on the TV in the mornings so Mary Ann had to knock on my door on 9/11. She told me a plane had flown into the World Trade Center. I didn't say anything; I just stood and shook until she raised her voice and said I had to come out of it. My memories of the city were deep.

Evenings in New York City fell into a pattern, one night the theater, one night a first-class restaurant, one-night Bridge. It was a life where there was no life with friends, relatives, hobbies, or a home, but at the same time both interesting and rewarding.

Then came the crossroad. I would either continue in Albany where my work situation had precluded me from settling into a life or making friends, or I would return to Buffalo. I opted to re- turn to Buffalo but, of course, I was in daily touch with the Albany office and Bill had been appointed to an administrative position to which I was subordinate.

So, the years flew. The office was doubling and tripling in size and so regional offices were emerging. Carmen, who was now in charge of the office, appointed me to supervise the New York City office, which by that time had 50 or 60 men.

Well, I had lived and worked many times as a woman in a man's world and I had the background in administration from Family Court. Consequently, even though I felt up to the job, I hated the situation I was in. I was alone in New York City and going to a hotel alone night after night. The men in the office were not "happy-campers" to think I had gotten the appointment. In any event, stories started to fly. I knew at the time I could have countermanded them but I didn't. So, by mutual consent, I returned to Albany.

I had to decide whether to make Albany my home for the foreseeable future or return to Buffalo where there was an opening. Because of the nature of my work, it took up 24 hours of my time each day, so I was not able to become part of the community in Albany.

There was a problem in that there was already one super- visor in the Buffalo Office but New York City had established a precedent of having more than one supervisor at a time. Addition- ally, the supervisor in Buffalo had failed the Civil Service Exam, so there was no question in my mind or the minds of my associates that he would have to be terminated.

November 1976

I returned to Buffalo and it was a confusing time. The apartment I rented fell through and I had to get one at the last minute. The change from the constantly exciting life seemed like death and was a terrible loss to adapt to. Mary Ann, the Hanover's and many other friends helped, but it was like I was cut off too soon.

When I was still in Albany, Carmen called a meeting one day. He announced that I had received a national award for my decision writing. My reaction was that it was a mistake. I asked him, "Are you sure that I wrote it?" He was stunned by my reaction, but he confirmed it by saying, "Yes I'm sure." I don't remember any of my colleagues—who were all male—congratulating me, but I don't think I would have expected it. Anyway, when the department started to increase several slots were approved by Civil Service. All the existing staff was promoted except for me and the one man who did not have the proper qualifications.

At least one of the men called Carmen's attention to the fact that promotions were being made before and after me, and I turned out that it was his close friend Peter Mullany who did not technically qualify for the promotion and Carmen expected heat if he promoted him.

A scheme was devised to promote me and Mullany the same day and the fact that I was appointed would take heat from Mullany. It worked. Most of the reaction seemed to center on my appointment. It happened that I enjoyed hearings so much I really did not seek the appointment. Although the unfairness of passing me over was patent—I never sought it.

Well in Buffalo, we all had calendars for hearings and both the other supervisor and I finalized decisions. Since I enjoyed the work so much, I never complained, but then there came a time when a question arose as to the fact that my supervisory slot was in Albany and here, I was in Buffalo. I was amazed and wondered whether they planned to appoint someone to the other super- visor's slot based on the Civil Service Exam list rather than me. I was in contact with several friends in Albany who were watching the situation the way you would a ping-pong match.

One day when I was off the calendar I simply got on a plane and flew to Albany.

When I walked into the Albany office, I felt like a leper. Heads either swiveled or went straight down, but like "little Eva in the snow," I persevered and walked straight into Carmen's office. Peter Mullany was there and proceeded to turn in circles. It was so amazing that Carmen and I both started to laugh.

He acted as though my arrival was expected and calmly explained their position. Then I was told that they just were not going to comply with the Civil Service requirements to canvass the list, but rather they were going to keep the existing judge as a temporary. Politics had reared its ugly head. The fact was that they did not know, as they had not in the past, or worried, about what a woman could do about it.

I was in limbo and I had no support system to call on to remedy the situation. After much soul-searching, I decided to bring an action for discrimination. All my friends, who were so close, disappeared and I stood alone. I could not possibly have with- stood the pressure except for the fact that I was out of Albany.

I made an appointment with another lawyer, Grace, and asked her to represent me. She hesitated to take the case although she thought the discrimination was obvious, but she finally made up her mind to do so. When the complaint was filed in the Albany Office, the Counsel told Carmen to settle it. Carmen called me but I didn't receive the call so he reported back to the Counsel that I had refused to take his call and the matter went forward.

June 1976 to June 1983

I actually had thought when I brought this action, that regardless of how hard I worked, or how much I accomplished, or any recognition I got from any source whatsoever, that essentially, I was tolerated rather than accepted and considered fortunate to be allowed to do the work. I think many years of practice had taught me to keep my eye on the main chance. I was over 40, enjoyed the work immensely, and in terms of a lawsuit was fortunate to be out of Albany. I had no desire whatsoever to change my job, or my career.

What I really wanted was to retain this job to retirement, and it was only by legal action that I was able to do so.

Up until this point, I accepted the bad with the good, always staying focused on my own best interest, but now the department had grown and essentially—I was not going to be permitted to grow with it. Even *that* I could have accepted, except for the fact that you have got to determine at what point, you are damaging yourself by being, for lack of a better word, mistreated and not having the guts to do anything about it. The point had come for me to say I didn't accept this treatment. What's more, the law protected me now against prospective employers *who could yell through the intercom*, "**We don't want women!**"

The question was: was the law enforceable? The answer probably was—for all practical purposes—that it was "Mickey- Mouse." One might say "sub served" under it, was the ability to play cat and mouse. One Judge made the statement that he knew Mary Davey and he could not believe she would do such a thing as bring a legal action for discrimination. She always seemed like a nice person. Goldfedder, the erstwhile supervisor, was quoted as saying he would be willing to testify against me in any forum since I was given the same pay as men. I was, of course, in a Civil Service slot and I had been assigned the same work. I should be thankful I was accepted.

Long after the commencement of my action, Grace rep- resented another woman who was a lawyer in a discrimination action. She told me it was eerie talking to us because the facts were different, but our reactions were virtually interchangeable. I had known of the other action from a source other than Grace and it was hard in a way that it had a sense of being standard.

I remembered from my working days at Human Rights: a Black man coming in to file a complaint. He had gone to a barber who told him he did not cut Blacks' hair. The complainant was not in the least upset and did it almost perfunctorily. He was not even interested in having to waste his time at a hearing if it could be avoided. The barber was contacted and he knew his license was in jeopardy.

He cried, misunderstanding, but was perfectly willing to accept whatever requirements were made of him to right the wrong. End of case.

Believe me that handling of a matter of sex discrimination could in no way be equated with racial discrimination. I never experienced one situation in which the accused took the position that there was an absolute entitlement to discriminate racially. I am not in any way suggesting that it was not the private opinion of many. What I am suggesting is that long after sex discrimination was included in the law, not only did the accused blatantly and without any effort at cover consider it justified, but *so did the judiciary.*

It was a long painful experience. I attribute psychoanalysis with giving me the stability to get through it. What I had learned was that while enduring pain, disrespect, hurt, and just plain meanness, one can go on appreciating the work, your home, your friends, your vacations, your family, the holidays, your birthday, a beautiful warm Sunday morning, the blizzard of '77, the fascination of a presidential assassination. We human beings are un- believably resilient if we will just let it all happen. As Hildegard of Bingen said, "All will be well and all will be well and all manner of things will be well."

So, the fat was in the fire. At first, the department was afraid of repercussions as was I, so the whole thing was tentative and I just went on with my work as usual. The Division of Human Rights was dilatory beyond belief. They seemed to have a policy of not making waves. Grace brought the matter before the Supreme Court. It was almost as though the action was not comprehended. I don't think it was. Then started the harassment . . . I would receive my files with a note attached which said "prick."

The most unprofessional and blatant was when an Erie County employee appeared to represent her grandmother in a Medical Assistance case. The woman was clearly over the asset level and so did not qualify. I tried to be as kind in my explanation of eligibility levels, but the woman would have none of it, looked at me with clear resentment, and commenced crying.

When the hearing was over, I told the representative from Erie County that the woman was going to make trouble. Having been challenged I was able to ferret out the scheme. She was an operative and was sent through a politician's office. The politician was a "rabbi" and I was intended to be a "fall-guy." I wrote letters to my legislators accusing the people involved of trying to use undue influence with respect to a judicial decision.

I wrote to the Personnel Department of Erie County to ascertain if the employee who represented her grandmother had approved time off from her job and if the time was charged against her earned time off.

I was in the office at lunchtime a few days later when the telephone rang. It was one of the employees in the Assemblyman's office. She did not realize who she was talking to so I heard a quaking voice refer to the incident and ask, "Is it over?" I knew I had won that round but was sure the troops would simply regroup.

The one dread I had was being assigned for a period to either the Albany or NYC office. The whole matter was so dicey; I don't think Carmen or Peter wanted me to be in the Albany office for a week—but dread of all dreads—I opened my schedule-one week and found myself assigned to the New York City office.

What to do? Nothing! Get on the plane and go. Oh, how times had changed from the days of the "Mod Squad" and the fun and camaraderie. I would be alone assigned there for the week. When I arrived, first, there was a problem of a hearing room, then of equipment, then getting the people to my room—then the wretch in charge of the calendar started swearing at me and calling me "Bitch." I tried unsuccessfully to report it but everyone turned their backs and refused to listen. So finally—in desperation
—I walked out.

I knew Bill Carr was in New York City and returning to Albany by state car that morning, so I telephoned him for a ride to Albany. By the time, he finished his business and I had gotten back to the hotel to check out, it was lunchtime. I told him this one's on me and that I wanted to go to the Plaza. I would go there for brunch if I was in New York City for the weekend.

We went and had a delightful lunch before returning to Albany. The experience reminded me of the story of the monk who slid off of a precipice. He grabbed on to a root. He looked above him and realized he did not have the leverage to climb back up. He looked below him and the drop was 1,500 feet. He was desolate but then he looked at the root he was holding. It had a bright, ripe cherry on it and he ate it. It was so sweet. So was the Plaza . . .

Bill drove me to the airport in Albany and I flew to Buffalo. The next day I wrote decisions until lunch and then met with the union representative who had charge of matters concerning professional employees. When I told her what happened, she said I must return immediately to my assignment in New York City and file a grievance.

Additionally, I could fully expect to be terminated for leaving the assignment. All of the above happened, so now I had another area of litigation going.

Little Mary Sunshine had to get back on the next plane and return to the scene of the crime. Let me tell you if you don't happen to understand, that one must muster up all of the guts one has to walk back into this bastion of males all able to make brownie points by abusing you and proceed to get to work. Strangely, though, this particular incident had climaxed. Since no one, myself, or my supervisors could have anticipated my reactions, no plans had been made for the next step and I just quietly held hearings for the rest of the week. Of course, I was alone and treated like a pariah by my colleagues, but what the hell; I couldn't expect everything in life.

My litigation dragged on year in and year out. Carmen left the department and was replaced by Peter. Peter never did meet the Civil Service qualifications for anything, so he proceeded to staff the department with lawyers who were younger and routinely promote them over the older more experienced lawyers who were Civil Service. The department had become a hotbed of discontent where now my sex discrimination complaint was followed by male age discrimination complaints.

Peter would end up periodically in a treatment facility for alcoholics, but he would return as mean as ever.

One attorney in New York City who said something to displease him got down on his knees to beg him not to fire him peremptorily. Peter would not budge. I can usually figure out something about a person that kind of explains their condition to my satisfaction. Mullany was the exception. His conduct was unbelievable, underhanded, and mean, but at least I wasn't alone insofar as his horrible treatment. Others who suffered at his hands would call me to share the misery. So, before I was through, we had also tried the EEOC and found it completely inept. It seemed as though in the '60s there was a stomach for alleviating this type of situation, it had a hiatus in the early '70s. I even had to have a private attorney to handle my matter that involved the union, and in the final analysis, it was he who said he thought I was fortunate to have reached retirement age and the best outcome for me would be to take my pension.

May 1981

Well, I got married. How did that all come about? My friends, when I told them I was to be married would say, "To whom?"

The years that I was involved in the discrimination case were tough years. I did the usual things of life in that I bought an apartment in The Campanile—, which I really loved. I took vacations but usually no further than Chautauqua. I did the culturals—mainly with Mary Ann—but had only occasional and minimal male interests. I spent time with Grace and her son, John, whom I enjoyed watching develop. I was intensely interested in his well-being, but Grace was fed-up to such an extent with the prolonged litigation that our friendship did not really survive.

Mostly though, I had an underlying worry and anxiety. The rest of the Albany office also was a hotbed of turmoil, which made it possible for me to maintain some working relationship with, among others, Bill Carr. A lot of our decisions were based on policy and this did not filter down to the Buffalo office. So, I was able to keep current with my relationship with the Albany office.

Bill was over the supervisors administratively and occasionally came to the Buffalo office. One time he told me that his wife was seriously ill.

He was completely broken up about it. It happened about the time my father died, so I too was grieving.

It looked as though Daddy might not be able to continue alone in his house in Canada. I had held hearings in a senior home in Buffalo where the residents seemed especially happy. I spoke to him about the possibility of living there and I got an unqualified, "No!" I offered to buy a duplex to share it with him, but again he was disinterested.

Both Ellen and Jack had young people in their homes as well as a family life and I guessed that that was more appealing to him. However, when he was about to get on a plane in Washing- ton, he dropped over dead of congestive heart failure. It was said when he was born that his birth was under a heavenly star and it was believable. He celebrated Christmas at 94-years old, and not ready to give up his independence so he simply dropped over dead.

Chapter Eight ♡Bill

To live in this world
You must be able to do three things:
to love what is mortal:
to hold it against your bones
knowing your own life depends on it;
 and, when the time comes to let it go.

—*Mary Oliver*

Well, Dear Diary, I'm at Mt Carmel. I came here largely to address you. At least I have the pages in order and I think the subject of the night should be . . . "Bill." Bill was such a wonderful friend. If you are the only women working with a group of men, it's so important to feel real friendship, but I must hasten to add that most of the men I worked with at that time were caring, thoughtful, and helpful people.

My father died unexpectedly and within a week, I was talking to Bill on the telephone. He told me that his wife was seriously ill. She died soon thereafter, and Bill was in the Buffalo office shortly after that. He didn't say much, but it was obvious he was grief-stricken. We talked on the telephone concerning business, but I did not see him again for about a year.

He told me thereafter that many people had tried to arrange dates with women, but he wasn't interested. We spent some time together and then he partially retired. He had all the time in the world to come to Buffalo, and he did. On his return from Buffalo to Albany, he drove to Harold Wass's farm with the intention of introducing himself, but fortunately, for him, he changed his mind first.

After about a year, he proposed to me. He suggested that we keep our money separate as I was still too young to retire, nor did I have any entitlement to a substantial pension. By contrast, he had qualified for a satisfactory pension and felt satisfied with his financial future. My answer to him was that I felt unsure about marriage, but if I did, the circumstances would be that his income would be ours and my income would be mine. He agreed.

Bill had 11 children and 24 grandchildren alive when we married. I had met them in Albany and had been treated most respectfully. I expected to be a very good stepmother for whom I would be most appreciated, but I was naive. Bill had two sisters who were nuns and for that reason, he didn't want his family notified about our wedding plans since I had a living husband, which precluded a Catholic ceremony. I had been very reluctant to marry, but I knew it was either that or lose Bill and there was no doubt that I loved him.

So, we were married in the Grotto of the beautiful backyard of the Campanile. Mary Ann and Don were the witnesses and Mary Ann Killeen performed the ceremony. Mary Ann's parents were there, as were my cousins Loretta and Ernie Hanover, and we had dinner at the Rue Franklin. Bill and I went to Niagara-on-the-Lake to spend the night and then to Toronto. I had told no one at our place of employment that we were being married, so we only had the weekend after which Bill had to return to Albany to deal with some unfinished business. I returned to work.

A few weeks later, we took a trip on the Delta Queen, which was our honeymoon. I found the adjustment to marriage unbelievably hard after I had lived alone for so many years. Bill heard at church about a Marriage Encounter Weekend and we decided to go. We both found it very helpful, but in any event, we were very dedicated and only troubled with the day-to-day inter- actions. We had no disagreements about money, religion, where we would live, or even politics.

We spent a lot of time traveling to Albany to see his family and having them visit us at our house in Canada. I retired after we were married for about two years but was very reluctant to retire so Bill was quite an incentive. There was much of the United States that we enjoyed seeing and always (of course), enjoyed time together in New York City. I really wanted a condo in Florida but Bill thought it would stop me from traveling so we limited ourselves to visits. I knew he was right.

In 1984, I found an article about, "The Universe," a ship that was sponsored by the University of Pittsburgh and voyaged around the world. It was $10,000 per person and I figured another $5,000 each for land tours, but Bill thought it was too much money. We had been on a wonderful Elderhostel trip to Australia and New Zealand and Hawaii, but I said watch me accumulate the money—and I did.

We were accompanied on the voyage by Paul and Jo Harrington. Paul was the little "colored-boy" in the Mod Squad when we worked in New York City. He developed an unbearable temperament. Our trip was three months of magic. There were constant activities on shipboard. We had a full college faculty and experts to speak on the countries we visited. We had a variety of athletic activities and a bunch of students doing calisthenics on deck; it looked like a kaleidoscope of butterflies.

This was the start of my long study of Buddhism, which was a philosophy Bill so graciously shared. We got off the ship in Portugal the first day and got lost in the Jewish quarter. To me it was hilarious, but no one else thought it was funny.

We loved every bit of Europe and went to a restaurant in Greece that I had found reviewed in the New York Times even though it was an hour cab ride out of town. There were fishermen catching fish and bringing it immediately to the restaurants where you could choose your lunch. The men stood in a row saying, "Try my fish," and we loved it.

By the time, we reached Istanbul I was in the mood for both buying and a bath. I had studied Prayer Rugs before I left and purchased a Hereke for $1,100.

To my surprise, however, when I came home Bill looked it up in a book. It was listed for $20,000. I guess that could be called a fish story, but the facts as I lived them are correct.

The Turkish bath was the zenith in any unusual experience to me. It does make one seem a little light headed to attach so much importance to a bath on a trip around the world, but I have to say nothing in my memory compares to it.

Jo Harrington accompanied me. She had no desire to go but was always ready for what might be fun. We went to a large unattractive room that looked like something you might find at the "Y." We were told to remove our clothes—all of them including our shoes—and were given wooden clogs. We marched in line. I felt like I was in the kind of line up you see portrayed in Concentration Camps. We went into a large room at regular intervals. There was a pad with a woman sitting on it—a very large woman with exposed breasts wearing only a black diaper. She looked like a Sumo Wrestler!

Jo and I rather hovered in a corner and we were joined by a very elderly looking woman. I said to Jo, "I thought it was only to be our group here." Jo stared at her then looked at me and said, "She's your next-door neighbor on the ship; she just doesn't have on her wig or teeth." I drew further into myself.

Then we witnessed the operation. One of the Sumo Wrestlers grabbed a woman, threw onto her pad, and pummeled her. Then she poured water over her and took her back to her spot. All I can remember is the shock. It didn't seem to really hurt, but it was also invasive. Half the time I just sat there stunned.

Then we went to a little restaurant, which was adjoining. I did not recognize the food but did the best I could. It was absolutely and unforgettably delicious. We returned to the ship where Bill and Paul were waiting for us. I went right past them and said I had to lie down. I went right to sleep.

When I awakened, I had a feeling of being more alive and well than ever before in my life.

I thought pirates were only in romance novels, but as we went through the Suez Canal there was a watch for them—they seemed to think of everything. I had been in Cairo in 1959 and now the city looked like a sprawled mud heap. I couldn't believe the difference. So off we sailed to India and the ship's doctor said that half the ship would be carried back sick from the food. We tendered in the harbor and had to crawl over sacks of potatoes to reach land and be assisted by our Asian crew herding us back on deck.

They were small men, I felt like a giant as they helped me up the side of the ship. We took a cab ride with Jo in the front seat. She was terribly restless and I eventually discovered why—there was no floorboard. Everywhere you had to step over bodies to walk a block. When we got to Delhi Agra, rickshaws took us to the Taj Mahal. Bill refused to get into one saying he would not have a human being carrying him. The rickshaw drivers foresaw a big tip and crowded around to get him as a passenger.

I bought enough stuffed animals in Korea to supply the 24 grandchildren and learned to love the Buddhist chanting in Taiwan. When we reached Sri Lanka, I considered it the most beautiful place in the world. First, we spent an afternoon with Arthur Clark and on another day went to the Nun's Island.

Our trip to Hong Kong and China was eventful. We went to a Catholic Mass in a church that had just re-opened. When the priest saw us, he invited us to his home and we tried to converse in spite of the language barrier. As we left, we were followed by a card-carrying Communist who interrogated us. I don't scare easily
under these circumstances, but I sure didn't want to end up in jail in China. I guess it was good we were coming from church—the Lord provided.

Our last stop was Japan where we were met on the dock by a Blue Grass Band playing "Walkie Talk." We were told we could drink the water and eat everything. I celebrated by eating scallops. We had a reservation in a Roya Kahn and were told there was unisex bathing. Poor Bill hurried to get through dinner to find I was the only taker. Something I had for dinner made me sick for the first and only time.

We departed Japan leaving several students behind. They forfeited their senior year in college. The father of one offered
$20,000 for the ship to turn around and pick him up. The Pacific proved to be a difficult ocean to cross, but the sight of land leading to home was a joy to behold. We did it and we were glad.

The next year Bill and I took a trip to Africa, our last big overseas adventure. Bill had such a capacity for enjoyment.

Basically, he was sick, but he still roused himself over and over. He loved seeing the amazing wildlife, the exotic landscape, and the unique people. Our safari vehicle was bumpy, but we thoroughly enjoyed the trip.

Bill was not well! He had a complete physical in October and we left for Florida in January. Bill had always just loved our house on the Niagara Blvd. in Fort Erie, Ontario. Winston Churchill remarked that it was the prettiest street in the world and we both agreed with him.

Before we left, Bill and I had an altercation. I wanted to drive to Florida by way of his daughter's home in Maryland. Bill's first great-grandchild, who's part African-American and was born out-of-wedlock (*isn't that a funny old-fashioned term*), had been born just a couple of months previously. His daughter did not favor our plan to come, but I was absolutely determined. *Bill even went as far as neglecting to renew his prescriptions so we had to delay the trip.*

When we arrived, Claudia, his granddaughter, came to his daughter's with the first great-grandchild. Bill took the baby in his arms and his expression was purely spiritual. He looked transfixed with a type of peaceful joy. Bill died before any other opportunity to see that baby, so it gives me great joy that I was so determined.

We rented a charming little house in Florida overhanging the water and spent many happy days with his son and daughter-in-law and their two children, but it was also obvious Bill was sick. We went to play bridge one day and he said he had to go home. He asked if I would tell the director I was sick. I did.

I tried to persuade him to have the car driven back so we could fly back, but he wouldn't go for it. We started out one morning but he stopped the car, turned around and threw himself on the bed. The ride home was one from hell. The next day after we got home, he permitted me to telephone his doctor, but not ac- company him to the doctor's office. He was admitted to the hospital and died three weeks later. When I first notified his family of how sick, he was no one believed me, but before he died, he saw each of them and so was able to say goodbye.

The last day I saw him he had been put in restraint because he was throwing himself out of bed from pain. I spoke to him and he seemed to ask me for something, but I was so upset I couldn't understand him. Thereafter the doctor came in and said I should leave. He described Bill's death by the term "Lazarus Death," meaning he repeatedly died only to come back, and he said I should no longer sit and watch it. Kathleen stayed, but Bill died toward morning. I was half-awake when the telephone rang. *I felt a breeze pass over the bed the very moment of Bill's death.*

One day much later Kathleen told me that she had under- stood what her father had said. He had looked at me and said, "I love you." After that, he never spoke again. Her generosity to me was beyond belief. Every Sunday I'd throw my back out and crawl to the doctor on Monday. I was so lonely it was palpable. I not only dreamed of Bill, but I also started dreaming of Harold Wass, who had been killed in an automobile accident two years after Bill and I were married.

I was very thankful at this point that Bill had insisted on my learning to play duplicate bridge. We always had company every weekend when Bill was alive and now there was no one. I was not only emotionally sick but physically sick as well. I could see no redeeming quality to the suffering and felt that my life was over—I wanted it to be.

There was a memorial service at Fordham. Bill and Peggy went to New York City with me. It was even worse than being alone because now I felt that I was catching others in my depress- ion. I have no recollection of anyone, anytime, anything that helped me in the slightest except the passage of time. I would go to an area of the church on Sunday where I could be by myself and quietly weep. The only insight that came out of it was "me next." I never wanted to go through it again, but such was not my fate.

For five years, I continued in my house on the Niagara Boulevard. Ellen lived in Canada, but unfortunately, our relation- ship was strained much of the time. Through a program at Saint Michael's church, I had made friends with several women who attended the church, and my cousins, who also lived in Canada. They were very active in the church and community and were a great comfort.

I served on the board of a state of the art "YMCA" and I attended "Overeaters Anonymous" meetings held there where I met several friends who spun off with me into a spiritual group. It was perhaps the one time when Mary Ann was not helpful, but as usual, we did not question one another. What eventually emerged was that I was blessed by a time when I had health, financial resources, and found life very interesting.

It started with four friends from O A deciding to make a spiritual study. After Bill and I got back from our trip around the world, I found a group of mediators to join. Bill had always been most supportive of my spiritual endeavors, but he didn't choose silent meditation. On shipboard, he was happy to study Buddhism more or less as an abstract subject, but now, the plot really thickened in the story of my spiritual journey.

Bill never looked to the left or to the right as a Catholic and the one regret I had after he died was that knowing he was facing imminent death; I did not ask if he still felt as sure with respect to the hereafter as he had all of his life. I am confident he would have willingly answered me, but I never got around to asking him. However, I did not forget to put the fact that he was a member of the Fordham Glee Club in his obituary. He always said it was his proudest accomplishment!

Chapter Nine ⚢ Mary Ann

You don't have crazy anymore, my dear—
 We all know you are good at that.
But now my dear please retire
 from all the hard work you do
of bringing pain to your own
sweet eyes and heart.
Look into a clear mountain mirror
and see the beautiful ancient dance,
The beautiful ancient dance,
and the divine elements you always carry inside
 that infused this universe long ago
with sacred life
and join
with the eternity of existence
now.
—*Hafiz*

    Oprah Winfrey has been alluding to the fact that she is not gay. It has given me pause. I felt the same way about Mary Ann— doesn't maturity dictate that you live your life and that your per- zonal choices are yours alone and no one else's business? Then why is it offensive to someone like Oprah who lives in such a sophisticated milieu to concern herself with it? But it is an affront that two women cannot have a deep emotional tie without it being sexual.

    Jeff Simon wrote a column on it in the Buffalo News and I didn't know what he was talking about. I do know that Doctor Lichtenstein indicated that my relationship with Mary Ann was quite unusual. I remember asking him how he thought it would end. He said that he did not know. I posed the question because it was such an all-encompassing relationship that I thought one or the other of us would tire of it. Each of us did after time, but the times never coincided. In fact, we spent so much time together that she felt the relationship would be altered in a manner negative to her when I told her I was going to marry Bill.

Bill had come to know me when we worked together in Albany and New York City and at that time, Mary Ann was not such an evident part of my life.

The relationship was a question to him, but one I felt he had to answer for himself and he did. When we were first married, she would call at inconvenient times, which disturbed both Bill and me. It was usually on Sunday afternoons. Gradually she formed the habit of going to her parents, which ended up being a great pleasure to all three of them. Then a shift occurred. Bill had no friends or family (Kathleen, his daughter, was totally independent and mostly unavailable) in Buffalo so in effect, there was no one to talk to. At first, I didn't notice, but then I would observe that often when I wasn't in the room there would be a tête-à-tête going on between Mary Ann and Bill. He had someone to talk to and share his disturbances with. It was the same relationship I had with Bill. If I was coming into the room and I heard such a conversation. I'd turn around and go someplace else. I was very glad he had that relationship and I never mentioned it to him. When he died, Mary Ann said that the grieving was not all mine, she also loved Bill.

And for all practical purposes, that's the way it went. She would not care for a friend of mine, but then with the passage of time, she would always end up liking my associates. I had problems with my family, and while Mary Ann would be sympathetic, she really cared for each of them and would always say so. Similarly, I would often disagree with her, but somehow, with the passage of time, I found that the people she liked would become simpatico to me.

Mary Ann came from a family where she had a very strong mother and a weak father. Her mother had been responsible for the running of the house—bearing and raising the children—but at the same time toting that barge and bringing in a paycheck. Mary Ann was the middle of three sisters and lived in a house of two flats. One was occupied by Mary Ann's family and the other by her uncle, his wife, and two girls.

Lifelong, Mary Ann had an abiding love for one of the two girls, her cousin, Renee. At Christmas, Mary Ann and her cousin would go with their fathers to visit relatives.

The men thought it was amusing to allow the girls to drink from an early age and would bring them home inebriated. Today an experienced person would see that Mary Ann was a potential alcoholic.

She was exceptionally pretty and very popular in high school. Mary Ann learned of a weakness in her personality when she was elected president of her high school sorority. It turned her into an autocratic, dictatorial person—she could never handle authority.

She graduated from Alfred University and then saved enough money to go to Europe with two of her friends. They bought a car, got pick-up jobs, and spent months wandering around Europe. At that time, her conduct was considered most unusual. Mary Ann was always very attractive to men and that allowed her trip to be extended.

She never believed in paying for her own dinner. At the time she came to work for the County, where I met her, she was in her late twenties. She said she had tired of the dating scene and so gradually fell into a pattern of going with Don alone which lasted for the rest of her life. Don seemed crazy about Mary Ann at first, but with the passage of time the glow wore off and they fell into a pattern. It was only after Mary Ann died that Don told me that at one point, several years after the commencement of the relationship, Mary Ann asked him if he would marry her if she quit drinking. He evaded her while explaining that he was responsible for his mother.

Mary Ann started off our relationship by interfering with the running of my department. She was misusing her authority and I had to report her to the senior judge, Judge Niemer for whom she worked. It was her nemesis, misusing authority. At that time, the two-martini lunch was in vogue and it fit right into Mary Ann's way of life. I couldn't handle drinking at lunch, but we were active together in politics, so we took a trip together to Mexico. That was the commencement of what in many respects was a comedy team. When we landed in Mexico, we started talking about the airport for Anchorage to the consternation of many passengers.

We went for a drink in the hotel bar our first night and were invited to have dinner with a most attractive and somehow sinister man. Everywhere we went Mary Ann would get acquainted with the locals and then I would carry the ball. It was really the beginning of our lifelong friendship. We thereafter traveled to Europe where we met some folks in Ireland who introduced us to a "man- about-town" in England. He took us to Annabelles as well as the best restaurant in London.

Then we flew to Paris and met my cousin Paul and his girlfriend (they were from Georgetown and spending their junior year in Germany). They both looked completely European and found wonderful restaurants by osmosis. Mary Ann and I had taken to carrying on at one another. We were constantly topping one another in insults to the hilarity of all who listened and more or less entertained each other with it. When Paul drove us to the airport in Paris, he predicted that we would never last through our final week on the Algarve. We found the Algarve populated by a bunch of ex-Nazis and so we spent more time just touring and the nastiness subsided.

When we got home, I wanted nothing further to do with her, but that was always a challenge to Mary Ann. If someone didn't like her, she'd keep at them until they were worn down. After that, she was always in my life. We each were equally concerned with the well-being of the other. I think I was happier when something positive happened in Mary Ann's life than my own. She shared everything with me, her family, her home, as well as all the joys and sorrows that make up life.

Through the years, the only argument we had that was of substance, concerned her drinking. I was fortunate in that my stomach would not take any quantity of alcohol. I lived my life in Albany, Buffalo, and Canada, but there was always Mary Ann, and I always appreciated her. To truly love another person is to allow them to live their own life, and we always did.

After Bill died, I stayed in Canada for almost five years. Mary Ann lived at 83 Bryant Street.

I had suggested it to her and always thought it would be where I would live if I returned to an apartment. I attempted to purchase one, but it fell through and I ended up next door to Mary Ann. She didn't like it one bit, but, as usual, I didn't intrude on her life, and we fell into a pattern that, with aging, was mutually self-supporting.

For ten years, we lived next door to each other. They were hard years for her because she had been running the Board of the apartment house for a number of years and was unseated by a newcomer. It caused her several years of unhappiness and was parallel to a time when her drinking increased. Her looks became those of an obvious alcoholic. She still grabbed every opportunity that she had for happiness. For example, she loved the Phil-harmonic Orchestra, as well as every minute of time she spent with and cared for her mother.

Then there came a time when she started to hallucinate. I called A.A., Crisis Intervention, and her family but no one would help me. I finally called the psychiatric unit of Buffalo General Hospital. A nurse who was on duty spoke to me and she said firstly that I was taking the right action.

She said Mary Ann was a human being in desperate need of help and as another human being, I should help her. She then told me to again telephone Crisis Intervention and insist on help.

I called back Crisis Intervention and asked the girl who was denying me help what training she had. She said a year or so. I told her she was substituting her opinion for that of a psychiatric nurse with 27 years' experience. She then put me through to a counselor. The counselor insisted I first get in touch with her family again and ask them to work with Crisis Intervention. I didn't call again the one who had first refused to help, but rather her second sister. Her reply was that she and her husband decided to pass on this situation. I asked her to please take just one action and that was to talk to Crisis Intervention on the phone. She agreed and she was convinced by the counselor to meet her at Mary Ann's apartment.

When her sister and brother-in-law arrived, I left. Then the counselor arrived and I heard her go out into the hall and talk on a direct line to a psychiatrist. She said she didn't appear to be a danger to herself or any other. I followed the counselor back to the apartment and Mary Ann started shouting obscenities, swearing and threatening to kill me for interfering. I asked the counselor if she was going to leave her alone in that condition and she requested her sister and husband take her home with them. They reluctantly agreed and her brother-in-law was insistent that I should be handling it even though she was threatening me.

She spent the night with them and was up all-night hallucinating, seeing people come through the windows. No one slept. Her second sister met with her other sister, with me, and with Mary Ann and we all agreed that unless Mary Ann would go to the hospital for treatment none of us would continue a relationship, but in any event, her two sisters said they were through and they meant it (and for all practical purposes), they never helped again.

Mary Ann was admitted to the hospital and discharged after detox, and basically was unable to obtain any help. She couldn't seem to comprehend the A.A. program. My life was a whole series of these incidents for over a year, and essentially, I could obtain no help. I constantly felt that I would collapse from the strain.

My final episode was when I had obtained hospice care for Mary Ann and that night, I called them and said she needed help now. I was told they would come in the morning. I said if that was their decision, I couldn't take any more responsibility and that I was leaving her alone and going to go to my house in Canada for the night. A nurse then came and saw that Mary Ann had been walking on ground glass and the soles of her feet were in shreds. The hospice nurse said to me that her only wish would be to have a friend like me at the time of her own death. It helped.

My communication with Mary Ann was over. I began to feel that she was going to die and without any spiritual solace. I shook her awake and said to her, "Mary Ann, do you want to see a clergy person?" She sunk into the bed and said, *"Oh Gawd."*

We both laughed and that door was closed. The next day she sat straight up in her bed and said, "**I am going to die**." It was like an observation that she was amazed at, but she lay back in bed with no signs of distress.

These were the last words I heard Mary Ann utter. Mary Ann died five days later with her two sisters at her bedside. There was never any doubt in my mind of Mary Ann's love for me, so I was very happy to have her sisters there at her side. It befitted a person who never held a grudge against anyone in her life.

Catherine Doherty is quoted as saying that all of her life she tried to go just one day without thinking of herself and that if she accomplished it, it would be to have accomplished love. If I ever have known a person who could have spent a day thinking only of the well-being of others, it was Mary Ann. She was un- surpassed in her gift of thoughtful love.

Mary Ann's funeral was everything to which she was entitled. Someone said to me, "Who will come?" I said, "I will. Don will. Rene will." Then out of the blue, my cousin Sarah said she would come and bring her flute, and if that wasn't enough, her brother Paul flew in from Washington to play his guitar and sing. My niece, Mandy, also flew in from Denver, Colorado. All for a graveside service.

So we had pretty poems, beautiful music with Mary Ann's nephew's wife singing The Lord's Prayer a cappella and many spontaneous kind words. Brother John Crocker conducted the service and he really outdid himself for Mary Ann. My niece and nephew wrote condolences to me and I could hardly believe the caring. The services started with a Taize chant of, "Jesus Re- member me until I come into the Kingdom," and ended with the hymn most appropriate to Mary Ann, namely "When the Saints Go Marching In."

Chapter Ten   ☐   Mother

The loss of an earlier memory is irretrievable
and must be grieved and mourned,
but the gladness is the discovery
that life continues to unfold with meaning,
with connections of significance.
                                              -[Unknown]

    So now, I had work that I really liked, but Mother was sick. When I mention my mother's name, she is remembered by all who knew her as a splendid out-going human being. She suffered in her early life as a result of not having a mother and it saddened her whole life.

    From the time she left the convent, my mother was brought up by her educated aunts, so she lived in an intellectual, affluent, but somewhat loveless home. She had one long-term boyfriend, but he never wanted to marry her, so she took the chance she got by marrying my father, and as far as their interpersonal relation- ship, it worked out to be a loving marriage. I think she was over- whelmed to find herself with three babies eighteen months apart and no adequate means of support, nor a house of her own in which to raise them.

    She probably was depressed to a greater or lesser extent for many years. Mother had extreme compassion, but this meant stretching her income because she had all the stray relatives living with her family.

    What was expected of her during the war years was un- believable, but she went ahead and shopped with food stamps, cooked for nine people, and taught boys with cognitive issues. Mother loved her boys and was a real sergeant when it came to protecting their interests. She also had an ear and time to listen to the myriad of teenagers that hung around our house, and to her they were all welcome. When, finally, we were a nuclear family and then there was the empty nest, I think Mother and Daddy were quite compatible and seemed to live a happy life.

I was with her when she had her first seizure. Mother had never been sick in her life so it was hard for all of us to believe. When she knew she was going to die, she told me that she felt that she had everything life had to offer, but she had a dread of leaving Daddy alone. I answered her by saying he was so help- less he probably would not live six months after her. She seemed relieved. He lived 20 years independently and seemed to enjoy every minute of it.

A friend of Daddy's visited, and Daddy proceeded to ask— within earshot of me and Mother—how it was to meet women as a widower. Mother raised her eyes heavenward, but, thank God, we both saw it as humorous. Since he could not drive, Daddy walked to take the bus every day to see Mother at Roswell until the day she died. Then he said, "It's finished."

He suspected many women of having their eye on him for the avowed reason that his house was free and clear, but he never reciprocated the interest. Particularly in my advanced age, I am aware of how influential my mother was on my life and I remember her with love and gratitude.

One afternoon I was driving her on Elmwood Avenue when I looked at her and saw her face going up and down and she was unable to speak. After a few minutes, she was able to say aspirin and a glass of water. I stopped at the drug store. My cousin Jack Quigley was in the store, and I told him what happened. He said if it were his mother, he would get her to a doctor. None of us were ever sick so we had no family doctor, and besides, Mother lived in Canada. I telephoned the office of the husband of one of my classmates and he told me to bring her in. He said he thought she had a stroke and told me how to proceed I took her home and she lay on the couch. The whole family seemed to deny that she was actually sick. Thereafter, she lay on the couch and she proceeded to have a seizure. We called a doctor in Canada, and when he arrived Daddy asked him to take his blood pressure first, as he thought to deal with Mother's condition made him sicker than her. The next week or so Mother remained in bed and I stayed to care for her. She was most demanding. The doctor had said that she was to have no enema under any circumstances because it could cause further seizures.

Mother enlisted Ellen's help to have an enema anyway and never told me about it. It relieved me of the terrible responsibility that I felt, and from then until Mother died, Daddy and Mother bumbled along in the little house together.

As the summer wore on Mother could play one of us against the other and essentially do as she pleased, but I was unwavering in my support for her to get a diagnosis. I got a referral to a neurologist from Doctor Lichtenstein who put her in the hospital. She could not stand the bars on the window and told Ellen to come and take her home.

By this time, everyone in the family was telling me I was making her sick while I continued trying to find a doctor to help her. Mother and Daddy's oldest friends had a brother-in-law who was an internist. He saw Mother and called me in and asked me to take her to my apartment or he would have to put her into the hospital. It was the hardest decision I ever made in my life, but I said she would have to go into the hospital. I could not withstand the family friction and at the same time knowing that, Mother, in her wiles, would play one off against the other.

Mother had a grand mal seizure and was scheduled for immediate surgery. The doctor came down from surgery and said she had the most serious type of malignant tumor on the brain and then turned to me and asked if I had arranged for nurses. Because I was the youngest, I would wonder why I was singled out. I began my quest to find nurses, but it was a holiday weekend so there were none available. To help out, Jack brought Joan in and I spent the night with her.

At this point, we were told that Mother would need round the clock nursing care and no one had the money for that. Jack flew to Buffalo so that we could have a family conference about money. I remember getting so mad, I was ready to hit someone with the fireplace poker.

Doctor Lichtenstein suggested Roswell so I ran it by Doctor Brock. He said they don't take nursing patients but he would call for us. Roswell was studying Mother's type of tumor so they agreed to take her and it looked like we could have peace. How- ever, there were still additional hoops to jump through. The neuro- surgeon wanted to do a second surgery on Mother.

When asked, he said it might prolong her life another couple of months. I was thoroughly upset, so Ellen agreed to ask Mother if she would agree to surgery.

She was totally competent and answered; "No!" she had been through enough. Daddy wanted her alive as long as he could have her and Jack was interested from a scientific point of view, but my interest was Mother. Doctor Owen telephoned me, and I told him that surgery to prolong the life of a dying patient was contrary to Catholic teaching, and Mother had been a Catholic all her life and she objected to it.

The Chief Judge of the Court of Appeals was a brother to my godmother and my mother's closest friend. I wanted to try to obtain an injunction to stop the surgery, but I just did not have the stomach to go into court to oppose my father and brother and so the surgery went forward.

Subsequently, it was decided that Mother was in a sufficient state of remission to return home. I went in the day she was to be discharged and found that she had fallen out of a chair she was tied into. The head nurse spoke to me and I questioned the decision to discharge anyone in her condition to the care of an elderly man. She asked me if my father would abuse her. I said "No." She replied, "Your mother is dying and she would like to go home. If she doesn't happen to eat right or get bathed on time it all matters little if she can be where she wants to be, with whom she wants to be."

I will say Mother really seemed happy at home. One day I was there on my lunch hour and her face was in her plate of food. Daddy lifted it out and they went on eating. C'est La Vie Archi. I had to remember the words of the nurse. Mother died in May so she lived ten months after the first surgery. We gathered in my apartment to talk to the undertaker. He shook hands and offered condolences to my father and said he would ask a few questions. My father answered him by saying he could not speak English. I immediately commented that if he didn't speak English he couldn't speak because he didn't know any other languages. Then my father said to ask me the questions, that I am a lawyer and I know how to lie. Some friend of an aunt had an extra grave and that is where Daddy buried Mother.

May 1962

So now, I know what death means. Before Mother died, I thought nothing could be worse than her illness. After she died, it was worse. Daddy, who could not drive, following the unfortunate loss of the use of one eye, took the bus from Canada to Roswell in Buffalo every day to see Mother. In spite of her prognosis, he seemed to just enjoy every moment he could be with her, but when she died, he said, "That's it," and he started looking emotion- ally forward.

I was on a train coming home to Buffalo and thought I would have to tell Mother about the train ride . . . Oh the pain of the next thought—*Mother is gone*. I went to her grave Christmas Day and oh, what comfort it gave me. Ellen and Joe were in New York City and Daddy went to Jack's in Washington. I would have been alone in Buffalo, but my cousin Loretta Hanover invited me for the day that started a long chain of holidays at the Hanover's. It is really fascinating the way literally one door closes and another opens. Following Mother's death, Daddy had cancer of the bowel and I had a cyst the size of a watermelon in my breast. I went to the doctor's and said, "Is God trying to kill this whole family off at once?" Such was not the case, however; Daddy recovered and went on for another 20 years, and I am still here.

Chapter Eleven
Uncle Jim & the Hanover's

One of the unexpected gifts in my life was my relationship with my Uncle Jim and the Hanover's. I have always loved my Uncle Jim. He was such a funny fellow. He was a police officer and I guess for most of his career a desk sergeant. He was famous for letting the prostitutes out the minute the arresting officer would turn his back.

He was 10 or 11 at the time his mother died and he smashed every statue and religious picture in the house. He never thereafter believed in organized religion and would rave about there being no 3-in-1. However, he had a strict moral code, which had as its first requirement being clean inside and out (he preached a daily enema).

When we were growing up and had no car for a period, he would loan my father his car so we could go for a ride as a family. Every Christmas of his life, he would give me money when I was little, and cigarettes when older. He never expected anything in return.

The family whispered about his sex life. He could not contain himself with any good-looking woman in the room, but would giggle, joke and make a pass at her if possible. My mother always raised her eyes heavenward at his antics, but his poor beleaguered daughter suffered terribly from embarrassment.

The story was the aunts picked his wife. She was quiet, circumspect, and easily shocked. The only thing I could figure is that she probably had not any other opportunity and the aunts forced the issue for fear he would align himself with a loose woman.

One could believe that the marriage was never consummated, but they had one daughter, Loretta, and it's easy to believe that it was the result of one encounter, for they never lived together after she was born.

Loretta was 12 years older so I did not know her very well growing up, but the year my mother died, Ellen and Joe went to New York, my father went to Washington, and Loretta invited me for Christmas dinner.

Loretta was married to Ernie Hanover and had two boys, Paul and Mark. Also, always resent was Harry Ray (Loretta's cousin on the other side), Ernie's sister and her husband, and Lillian and Ed Levy.

They were perhaps the most hospitable people in my life except for my own parents, and I so enjoyed being with them. Uncle Jim played the fiddle, Loretta played the piano, Paul would play the guitar, and Paul's friend, Buzzy, the banjo. We would all sing and dance. Ernie never stopped encouraging one and all to have more to eat, have another drink, and as soon as possible start the music.

They lived kitty-corner from us during summers at Cres- cent Beach, another place where the children could usually be gone all day with no parental supervision. I say usually because there was an outside refrigerator stocked with beer, and one day Paul, Mark, and the other neighborhood children got curious and proceeded to drink enough beer to be falling down drunk. Everyone was horrified, but the scene was at the same time aw- fully funny.

The boys grew up and Paul joined the Marines. When he was sent overseas, his wife spent a year living with Loretta. Mark was in the Vietnam War and there was a map over the TV so we could always watch where he was. Obviously, he was terribly affected by the war both psychologically and physically, but he did survive it, married, and had two children, Laurie and Greg.

So, I had the pleasure, and it surely was a pleasure, watching the Hanover boys grow up, marry, and have their own families. Mary Ann and I met Paul and Marcia in Europe on our first trip and it was such a pleasure being there with students.

Because Paul's children spent so much time on vacations in Buffalo, I got to know them and love them. Paul, who is now with the CIA, is the oldest and is so intelligent and so caring (he played the guitar at Mary Ann's graveside service). Sarah, who bore three children, then adopted two more sick children.

The last adopted child is Hawaiian and named Mary Lillian. The youngest of Paul's children is Sean—my godson—who's in law school and in the process of changing careers.

The Hanover's were a close second to having my immediate family and I felt their support from the time my mother died. I was so touched the day my mother died when I was at the Hanover's and Mark, aged about 12, came down the stairs into the living room Nan." "I want you to know, Mary, that I always loved my Aunt

Loretta never really survived Ernie's death and so was the end of an era. Lillian is still alive in a nursing home and I still see her every month.

Paul Sr. comes to Buffalo with Marcia once in a while as do his three children and those are always among the brightest spots of the year. Mark's marriage broke up and we no longer see him, his wife or daughter, but fortunately, Harry and I still see Greg when he is home visiting his mother and sister. The Buddhists say live for the present moment and always stay aware that life is impermanent. The sharing of my life with the Hanover's was always joy in the present moment and though it's hard to have it impermanent, it was a very pleasant 60 years or so.

Chapter Twelve — Siblings

"Forgiveness is the fragrance the violets shed on the heel of the person who crushes it."

Change your thoughts, change your life.
—Doctor Wayne Dyer

My memories of my early years are all of idolizing Ellen and Jack. Ellen always seemed to me to be everything I was not. Intelligent, pretty, attractive personality by comparison to me as a boring, not too bright ugly duckling.

We were not good friends growing up. We did very few things as a family and less as sisters.

I first remember any real relationship with Ellen at the time when she went to New York City. Then and thereafter, when she married Gerry, we did evolve into friends, although we never thought alike. I just loved the activities of New York City, and our basic belief systems were similar when it came to pleasure.

Through the years, there were unfortunate disagreements and I do not think either of us basically knew the cause. We both drank cocktails and I don't think either one of us handled liquor well, but I also had the estrangements with Jack without alcohol involved.

Jack and I had a period of friendship when he returned from the war and he attended Canisius College. Again, he would limit any activities with me, but we did have a communication and our ideas were similar.

Through my adult life and stemming from infancy, I think there was reluctance on the part of both of my siblings to get too involved with me.

I think I had always had an unfulfilled dependency need. As is usual, it made me appear particularly independent—which was the facade I wanted. As a result of living with me from birth, it seems both of my siblings realized this unfulfilled need I felt; it was not one for which they would or could be responsible. My brother and I had a very pleasant conversation the day before he died and I have had an extremely pleasant relationship with my sister and her husband in recent years for which I am very grateful.

Chapter Thirteen ~ Willie the Cat

Bill's family had alluded to the fact that he did not like cats, so I resisted getting one. However, Mary Ann and I were out at her sister's farm one day and Joanne said one of her cats had just had a litter. She asked if I wanted one.

"No," I said, thinking of Bill's attitude and the extent to which we traveled.

Then by some circumstance or other, Mary Ann and I were out at the farm again within the week. Joanne was not home and I asked to see the kittens before we left. We went to the barn and I involuntarily picked up a kitten.
"She's coming home with me," I said.

Nobody challenged me and as I was getting into the car, I said to Mary Ann, "Here hold this," and gave her the kitten. I ran back to the barn and picked up a second one so the first kitten wouldn't get lonely.

We put them together in a box in the back seat and stopped at Brookfield Country Club on the way home for a martini to celebrate my new family. Joanne was mad when she got home because the kittens were too young to be weaned from their mother, but what did I know? And surely, she did not want them back.

Afterward, Bill said that he did not trust me to take responsibility of caring for the kitten, feeding her, or cleaning the litter box. Thanks a lot, Bill! I never asked him to take any of this responsibility from me.

Anyway, Willie was a docile cat and seemed very observant and intelligent like Bill. His family was angry that I called the cat Willie because that was what Bill's father had been called. Her proper name was Wilhelmina. Willie's sister was an absolute pistol, a live wire that seemed like she was made of electricity.

Their food dishes were in the summer room, which was two steps down from the kitchen. When I had them only about two weeks, I was going down the steps with their dishes, and Willy's sister ran under my foot. I stepped on her and started to scream. Bill picked her up and said she was fine, but he was just going to have her checked at the Vets. Then he kept on walking and put her in the Niagara River.

He came back up the driveway and said her neck was broken. I remember Willie sitting very still and observing the whole incident. I spent the rest of the day with her sitting on my lap and she didn't move. The postman came along and I spoke to him through the screen and told him what had happened.

"I'm sorry," he said, adding that he knew what a hard couple of days there would be for me. I could never forget how much I appreciated his understanding.

A couple of months later I pushed the button to close the garage door and Willie ran up the screen. Again, I screamed that I had killed the two of them. Bill did not appreciate histrionics, but just opened the garage door and walked away. Willie had succeeded in flattening herself out like a pancake and ran away from the door as fast as her legs could carry her—end of Willie and the door.

Willie was a joy in my life for the next 17 years. When we went on trips, Renee or Mary Ann would take care of her. Mary Ann reluctantly, and Willie was always glad to see us return.

After Bill died, Willie got out one day. She had had surgery to declaw her as well as to neuter her, but I didn't at the time understand the extent of it. Of course, as a result, she was a house cat. I was very worried one day after Bill had died when she got out and I found her standing in the driveway looking very worried herself.

I thought she wouldn't do that again, but a couple days later, when I came home from shopping there she was standing in the same place in the driveway. I was surprised that I didn't see her run past me, but on the other hand, I was deep in grief and not operating on all cylinders.

So, she ran in the house ahead of me. I put my groceries away and went upstairs to my bedroom. Willie was lying on the bed, and I thought I was losing it. I could have sworn she was in the living room, but we all know cats move fast. So, I took a big deep breath and went downstairs. My gaud, I saw her in the living room. I called Ellen and said I am losing it. I see Willie in two places at once.

She suggested that I look again and if there actually were two cats to telephone the SPCA. It took several trips up and down to convince myself that there were two cats in the house. Finally, I called the SPCA and told the man who answered my dilemma. I decided to try to put the cat in the living room that would run by me, out, and go on with my life. As everyone knows, you make a fool of yourself chasing a cat. So, I made a fool of myself until I gave up. The man from the SPCA who had answered either misunderstood me or I misspoke; the latter is more likely.

"Lady," he said, "we can't come out and chase a cat out of your yard!"

So, we sort of started off on the wrong foot. I told him that cat had gotten into my house.
Reluctantly, he said he would come over. By the time he got there, the cat was again sitting quietly and comfortably in the living room.
"Are you sure this isn't your cat?" he asked.

I assured him that the cat had come in with me and the groceries. He did the magic all vets do and had a hold of the cat in less than a minute. Willie had one white spot on her belly and as he picked her up, I said," That's my cat!"

At this point, he looked most anxious to get out but in the next breath, I said, "But there is another cat upstairs on my bed!" He looked ready to bolt—but finally—keeping well behind me, followed me upstairs. There sat the clone of Willie and by this time, he just asked for assurance that I did not have two cats as he ran with the one from the bedroom, downstairs and out of the house.

Mary Ann was around my house more after Bill died and she started to take an inordinate interest in Willie. She gradually got so that she would ask Willie questions and/or make observations and she would seemingly engage in conversation. Mary Ann was very confident that they were communicating and under-standing each other. You can't prove anything by me, but it sure seemed real.

Then Willie and I moved to 83 Bryant and next door to Mary Ann and I swear to the truth of this . . .

Mary Ann worked her wiles on Willie to become the most important in her life! It was unbelievable, but it was happening right before my eyes! Willie and I had been through so much together that at first, it made me mad, but Willie loved her attention and would look at me furtively after giving Mary Ann a loving glance.

Then I thought, what the hell, I can still see her every day so if they mean so much to each other, let her go live next door. Mary Ann can handle the food and litter.

Mary Ann agreed with alacrity and so Willie moved in with her. There were only two apartments off the hall, mine and Mary Ann's and so we kept the doors open so Willie could stroll back and forth at will. The only trouble was getting her in the right apartment at night, and being an intelligent cat just when you got sleepy, she'd give you a merry chase before you could get her situated.

We always felt very safe at 83 Bryant, largely because of the way the building was constructed. My living room was straight ahead, as you came through the door and to the right of the entry was a den.

One night I was sitting in my den when I saw a man who was a stranger walking in headed for my living room. "Could I help you?" I asked.

With great shock on his face, he looked at me and said, "I'm looking for the basement."

I told him that the elevator was behind him. "Just push the button for it to come up. Then get in and push basement," I said.

I waited a couple of minutes and then got up and grabbed my keys, locked my door and ran into Mary Ann's apartment. She was at the back in her bedroom talking on the telephone to Renee. I told her it was an emergency. We called the super who was an elderly man. He proceeded to go through the building with only a rock in a sock to protect him. We begged him not to do it, to leave it to the police, but he tried anyway.

As it turned out, he had been in Mary Ann's apartment and stole her handbag with all her earthly belongings from her social security card on forward.

She was devastated and I would hear her sob and say nothing like that had ever happened to her before. It made me feel like a punching bag that I was always having such unfortunate instances. Each time something happened to me, the police would say, "You handled that just right." I would always think I wish there was nothing to handle.

That ended Willy's freedom to run back and forth, but she did not live long afterward. Curiously enough, the responsibility came back to me when she was sick, but I didn't mind taking it.

She started to stay alone. I used to pick her up when I came home, lie down and put her on my stomach. I would still try to do that, but she wouldn't stay. It fascinated me that in at the point of death she wanted to be alone.

Mary Ann and I were out for Christmas dinner. When we came home, we found Willy dead. Mary Ann started to scream and I told her she had to stop. She was disrupting the whole building. She insisted we look for a vet. The only way I could calm her down was to tell her we would go over to Nancy's (a nurse and friend who lived in the building). So down we went to the foyer and walked across to the other side of the building where Nancy lived carrying dead Willy the Cat.

When we got there, she had her stethoscope ready plus other medical paraphernalia. She couldn't bear to tell Mary Ann that Willy was dead. I finally thought this whole event was bizarre and crazy. I picked up one of Willy's paws and let it drop.
"Can't you see she's dead?"
Then Nancy affirmed what I said, and Mary Ann just wept. She had apparently given some thought to the funeral arrangements because we immediately went back to Mary Ann's, wrapped her in a blanket and put her in the trunk of Mary Ann's car. Since Willie had lived most of her life in Canada, Mary Ann was determined that the vet who knew and loved her would cremate her and put her in an urn for Mary Ann to keep on her mantle.

The only problem was that we didn't know whether or not Canada Customs and Immigration allowed the importing of a dead cat. Mary Ann said she knew just how to handle it. I was nervous about it since I owned a house in Canada, and didn't want any trouble with Customs. Nevertheless, off we went to Canada with Willy in the trunk and her remains were on Mary Ann's mantle in a pretty urn until she died, and I buried it with Mary Ann's remains.

Chapter Fourteen Spiritual Journey

Every person, in the course of his life, must build—starting with the natural territory of his own self—a work, an opus, into which something enters from all the elements of the earth.

He makes his own soul throughout all his earthly days; and at the same time, he collaborates in another work, in another opus, which infinitely transcends, while at the same time it narrowly determines, the perspectives of his individual achievement:

The completing of the world.

—Pierre Teilhard de Chardin
The Divine Milieu

Upon reading my spiritual journey, my brother-in-law referred me to a poem, which doesn't say it all, but it says a lot.

Griffy the Cooper

The cooper should know about tubs, but I learned about life as well,
and you who loiter around these graves think you know life.
You think your eye sweeps about a wide horizon, perhaps,
In truth, you are only looking around the interior of your tub.
You cannot lift yourself to its rim.
—Edgar Lee Masters

Sitting here, I feel like I have been cursed by a need to know! I needed to know why Grandma said all those prayers. Am I a Catholic because Ellen was instructed to call me to Church? An action, which arguably saved my life. I was just beginning to have individuation; that would remain in my memory. Did the accident of sending me to a Catholic school save a major depression or disorientation?

Then—when again the secular was not handleable to me—the providence came to place me in a private Catholic school with nothing to back me but manipulative wits.

What was it that was offered in Catholic schools that allowed me to adjust in a way that I could not at public school? Was it merely an accident, class size, or some other objective reality—or was there a spiritual component that I longed for and needed?

My personality has always looked for the logical and so in high school when I was taught the five proofs for the existence of God, they fell short and I was disappointed; I think my dis- appointment was that the proofs were somehow cold and if God were to be found, God would be warm. If it were a cold god who would seek him? Someone desirous of harm and evil? We have another term for such an entity—Lucifer and/or The Devil—and I never felt any desire to know such an entity except insofar as a curiosity about why it would exist.

As a child, I certainly knew a judgmental God who was keeping very close track, not only of my deeds, but also of my thoughts. It was hard to figure that out because even figuring implied doubt and certainly doubt, if not evil, at least incurred a black-mark.

During daily life, it seemed like the easiest thing to do was just listen to what occasioned a good record and keep to it unless something else seemed like a lot of fun, such as talking back to Mother—which would result in plenty of satisfaction—and if you got all balled-up in this thinking, there was always confession to sort-of require God to erase all those bad marks. Of course, that too was a trial because sometimes it seemed you didn't have enough sins to tell and making them up—while practical—was not quite right and heaven knows withholding them could mean you still had them.

Of course, we knew darn well we were not straight on any of this, so as the saying goes, do the best you can and keep your bowels open.

There was also another dimension. I watched Sister Winfred and knew she had it all figured out and so thought it over carefully and decided to be a nun! I expected everyone to be deeply impressed by my call from God.

What a disappointment when I told my father and got possible approval. I was too hurt to continue thinking about it, but now I question was it all so simple or was there an actual spiritual attraction?

There was another problem connected with the whole thing. In addition to all the negative qualities God had, God was supposed to love you. I must have taken until high school to figure that out. I know you should honor your father and mother and mostly what I thought about that was that if you didn't it probably meant trouble. As to the question of love . . . No question in my mind that overall they were pretty good although I know once in a while they might not take my side if I was right or they might do something I didn't like, whether I liked it, or not, so you might say they sort of loved me and I sort of loved them.

Ellen and Jack were different. Pretty much, I think they were good to me in spite of my being the youngest and dumbest, but that didn't account for my attitude. I thought they were wonderful and I loved them whether they did good or bad.

I guess I was supposed to feel the same way toward God as I did toward Ellen and Jack, but I couldn't. The fact that I could not see God and that I had no proof God saw me put any question of love out the window, so now I secretly knew I was a hypocrite and a liar because if the occasion demanded it, I would mouth the words, 'God loves me' or 'I love God.'

Approximately, I am talking about the period between 5 and 15 and I was able to accomplish feats on my own that should have been beyond the ken of that age group and I submit they were actions that allowed me to develop in such a way that I could handle the vicissitudes of life and I am convinced there was an unknowable force at work. Well now, I am at Nardin being correctly trained to be a good Catholic Girl, and there is an added dimension to religion. We have retreats and no boring academic courses on retreat day, but the best part of all is you put your questions in a box and did not have to sign them.

We were supposed to be silent, but a group of us would get into the backyard and think up the dirtiest sex questions we could think of. For example, would you go straight to hell if you soul-kissed a boy or should you refuse to speak to a boy forever if he touched your breast? I had no boyfriend, so the questions were completely theoretical, but they were so shocking that they were really fun.

I remember the priest always answered them by pricking the balloon. He would give a thoughtful boring answer that made it seem that the question was not even dirty.

I was intensely interested in the proofs for the existence of God and the transplanting of organs, but the only thing I seemed to know to do with my interest was to bait the teacher.

Then came graduation and would you believe what those Nardin's gave us for a graduation present? It was a copy of *The Imitation of Christ* by Thomas a' Kempis, signed by our teachers. I could not believe that if they were going to spend some money on us, they could think up something quite as boring as that. I put it on a table in the living room because I was proud of having received the gift.

I remember asking my father if he thought Jesus Christ was divine. He was somewhat evasive and certainly acknowledged no divinity, but he did affirm the wonderful human being he was.

On the other hand, Mother always seemed to take great joy in going to Mass and I remember her saying that the Catholic Church adapts itself, so it meets its member's needs. I think she took great pleasure in the Catholic religion and the practice there-of.

So, it was very hard to find guidance on what to believe and what not to believe, but it is my opinion that that is always true for any thinking, intelligent person. It just might make it a tad harder when you get conflicting information from parents.

Ellen had left the church before I finished high school and Jack turned out to be a "hail & brimstone" Catholic.

He was always disgusted with anyone who misbehaved Saturday night and then went to Communion on Sunday. I always thought he was wrong that confession and communion were for sinners.

My freshman years in college I studied the Russian writers. I was so taken by War & Peace that I read it in one sitting. Tolstoy said, "where love is there God is" and demonstrated by his writing what he meant by it.

That's the first time I was ever really aware of a God I might like. I especially was interested in erotic love, but now, I could comprehend some meaning to Agape. Even my love for my cats was a special feeling and how wonderful to be able to engender it for all sentient beings.

Mother always seemed to have a quality of extrasensory perception, which intrigued me. It was like the qualities of some magician, a medicine man, and a fortuneteller. Hers was inexplicable but not extreme enough to seem fake.

At times in my life, I seemed to know things that were beyond guesswork, such as the exact amount for a settlement before it was stated, or the announcement of the death of Mary Ann's niece before I answered the phone, and even the breeze that went through the room when Bill died. They seemed to some extent religious experiences, but I was not sure they could not be explained without a separate dimension, so I just husbanded them without interpretation.

I was in school, working, or studying around the clock. I was continuously exhausted, but I made it a habit of listening to Rudolph Bing describe the Opera at the Metropolitan on Saturday afternoon as enforced relaxation. One Saturday afternoon I reached over and picked up a book lying on a table. It was my Imitation of Christ. I felt like I had entered a new world, a wonderful world, a true world.

I read it over and over and over. I prayed it every day. I did not try to analyze my reaction beyond that of extreme gratitude that I had found it. Then I learned that Mother had used it for prayers her whole life. I was catapulted onto a path where occasionally I would jump ship, but I had found the lead into my life's most meaningful journey.

Law School and working and romance took over my life and I don't remember much spiritually except for the fact that I always tried to conform my conduct to an imitation of Christ.

At one point, I tried the Unitarian Church because I thought their teachings were built on logic. It seemed much more, to me; like an academic course and I knew forever more that, I enjoyed ritual, incense, chanting and all the goodies that seemed to me particularly Catholic.

It will always be a wonder to me that I didn't develop an appreciation of scripture or the reading of the Word or the Proclamation of the Gospel. I don't know the answer to why. I spent 3 years in the American Catholic Biblical School and then did learn an appreciation, but earlier in Church, I had acquired the habit of letting my mind wander. The exception was the homily which if well done would really move me.

So, religion continued to play a very minor role in my life until my marriage broke up and to the best of my knowledge, I was not now considered a member in good standing. I had a Civil Annulment. Ellen was going to be married again and in a Catholic church and wanted me as her witness. I attended Mass at the Old Cathedral and asked a priest there if I would be permitted to. He told me I would and thereafter searched for me to tell me to go to the Marriage Tribunal since if Harold had withheld a previous marriage I would be entitled to a Catholic annulment.

I told him I did not plan to remarry, but he insisted that I could not know what was in my future.

I went to the Marriage Tribunal and never before or after in my life have, I been treated with such disrespect. The priest to whom I spoke mimicked a Nazi SS man in my evaluation. He said they had no place for liars or those who engaged in the evils of the civil court. He succeeded in getting me to hysterical tears. I went to see my cousin, Monsignor Loftus, and he said to stay away from them and so I decided I would forever (that was too long a time—I was destined to have one more encounter).

My beloved mother died. Monsignor Loftus said a beautiful Mass for her. While still grieving my father got cancer of the bowel. Fortunately, surgery cured him and he lived 20 more years. I also had my own cancer scare. I had a huge lump in my breast, which luckily turned out to be just a cyst.

It seemed for several years that the sky had fallen in but after these events subsided, I took a Caribbean Cruise with Elayne. We were seated at the Chief Engineer's table and had all sorts of male attention. I could not believe it but life was again fun. I was floating in the Mediterranean off the Island of Martinique when all separateness from the universe dissolved. I experienced a feeling of total bliss. There were no words to adequately de- scribe it, then or now, but I felt it was the first time I actually had a spiritual experience.

We went into the years of the Civil Rights movement and I was in the thick of it working for the New York State Human Rights Division. I began to appreciate the wonder of a Martin Luther King and the fact that he was a clergyman. I began to know of the Berrigans. I first became aware of theologians such as Dietrich Bonhoeffer. It was also noted that they were not all Catholics although some of them were.

I didn't tie their conduct to religion as such but I would always tie it to Christ. None of these leaders acted in any way contrary to my Christ and I would not have given much thought to whether, or not, I was talking about God or a loving God. I still had no feeling of awareness of a God who loved me.

At the time I was married to Harold, each of us paid scant attention to church even to the extent of being regular church- goers. When I met Bill, he was the typical cradle Catholic who never looked to the left or right and probably I would have just thought it meant a limited intelligence (Bill had an IQ of 157 and was a member of Mensa).

The fact that we could not be married in the Catholic Church was very difficult for Bill. After we were civilly married, he requested I go again to the Marriage Tribunal. In spite of my attitude, I felt I had to respect his wish. I told the priest I saw that I had heard Harold quoted from many sources as saying he had a marriage prior to mine.

He asked me how I thought he should proceed. I said the shortest distance between two points is a straight line so why not telephone him.

Harold had a farm in Varysburg and had retired there. The priest telephoned him and explained his reason for telephoning. Harold answered by saying I was his wife; he was being asked about the most painful part of his life and the Tribunal would hear from his attorney in the AM.

The priest asked if I had other suggestions. I had none! Thereafter Bill went again to attempt to pursue the matter and was told I was not his wife; he had no business concerning himself with me and not to come back. I, of course, was furious.

It was shortly thereafter that Harold was killed in an auto- mobile accident and I insisted upon going back to the Tribunal when I was not looking for any relief to tell the priest in charge how un-Christlike, rude, as well as ignorant I felt they conducted themselves. This kind of conduct was not Bill's thing but, in this instance, he accompanied me and supported me.

Our marriage was thereafter blessed by Father Weimer at the Newman Center and I was very thankful that Bill was at peace. I loved the Newman Center for attending church. Bill would have preferred the more traditional, but his first consideration was to get me to church and he wanted to attend the same one.

Throughout our marriage, religion was a very positive in- fluence. Bill knew what his beliefs were, but he never tried in any way to superimpose them on me. He found my search, my questions, my quest in general interesting and he would always do anything he could to help me.

Prior to marrying Bill, I had become interested in Zen, which I did not regard as a religion. I went to the Zen monastery in Rochester for a retreat and was told I could not return because my body construction was such that I could not sit lotus. The answer filled me with contempt so I dropped that for a while.

When Bill and I were first married, I would spend considerable time reading the Theologians like Hans Kung and trying to find spiritual direction.

I was always disappointed. As Miss Vale said about me, I could not be reached and I wanted so badly to understand. Bill would ask, what it was I sought so earnestly to understand, and I guess the answer was everything. I am convinced that for many, it is a simple matter, a gift in their genes, that they have a sufficient understanding to satisfy them and, God bless them, they are fortunate. But there are also those like me who have a heartfelt need—an itch that won't subside—to understand where we came from, where we are going, but most of all, love, which seems to be the primary mover.

And those of us require the prayer and assistance of all the rest of the universe because we have not received the simple gift but must spend our lives relentlessly looking for it.

I started looking down a different path when we took our voyage around the world. We studied Buddhism on the ship taught by Judith Simer-Brown whose name I just saw on the brochure for The Omega Institute. She was a very good teacher but "had the impression that she did not like the adult passengers in her class.

I have a picture of her standing with her hand on a chair and saying there is no chair. That seems so simple now. Sub- atomic particles are mainstream if not new age. I found the four noble truths and the eight-fold path easy in terms of giving you a set of guidelines and go live them.

I started to meditate with the group and it did not worry anyone that I sat on a chair. Judith said that faithful meditation would result in a mind-altering experience within six weeks. I did have a mind-altering experience, but not before years of meditation. I was sitting meditating, and I felt gripped. I felt as though I had the power to loosen the grip, but I made a conscious decision not to. I was having a "not of this world" experience for some unknown amount of time. When I came out of that heightened state my thought processes were gone. The mantra Maranatha just resounded throughout my being. If I was called upon to do something such as answer the telephone I could do so, but upon completion of the task, my entire self would again fill with my mantra.

We had started a little group to study ideas spiritual in Fort Erie. Upon my return from our voyage, I joined a John Main meditation group in Buffalo and had one study group in Fort Erie.

The day of our meeting, I announced my altered state experience and that I thought I was on a fast track to enlightenment. That was about fifteen years ago. I don't think I am on any track, but if I should be, it's a very slow one.

We studied various authors but the favorite of all of us was Tony De Mello. We did his meditations and exercises. One day I sat on the banks of the Niagara River with a friend who was not in the group. A la de Mello, I asked her to go back in the picture before her eyes. See the region before the white man came and before the road signs, etc. We talked for a while about the picture and she told me thereafter it was one of the peaceful experiences of her life.

De Mello told us to look for self-interest in whatever we did. We all protested concerning the number of actions we took out of the goodness of our hearts, but as per the agreement, each questioned the other until there was no more conceit left.

We went to the Redemptoristine Convent, which was beautifully located on the Niagara River for meditation, and so had many happy days.

I moved back to Buffalo five years after Bill's death and joined a meditation group led by Brother John Crocker. It was a snowy day the first time I went to a Saturday meeting in Clarence. I was now in my 60's. I was working on a life master in Bridge, and I tried to maintain my health through activities at the Jewish Center and generally was blessed with a busy life, but that first day I met Bob, and from that time until he moved to Florida two years ago, he was the most influential person of my life's quest.

I continued following John Main and as a result went to retreats given by Lawrence Freemen in Niagara Falls, Toronto, Florida, California, as well as New York City. I found him quite erudite and very Buddhist in his thinking, but it was always interpreted with a Catholic viewpoint.

I explored Vispassna meditation with Mary Jo Meadows and formed a personal relationship with her as well as attending her retreats at Mount Carmel. After Tony De Mello died, he was kept alive by retreats given by Jim Dolan. I attended two twenty years apart. In Buffalo, Sister Annabelle (the heir apparent to Thích Nhất Hạnh, a Vietnamese Buddhist Monk and Zen Master), gave a retreat and I also attended another one in Vermont. I spent a week with Thích Nhất Hạnh at the Omega Institute.

For many years, I went yearly or semi-yearly to the retreats given by Sister Jean Lavin in Erie, Pennsylvania. She had studied under a Zen Master who was a Benedictine Sister in Germany and thereafter under Willigis Jäger, a priest who is also a Zen Master.

My favorite priest was Father John Mergenhagen who was always so sincere, so talented, and so humble.

I have neglected to mention the gurus that I studied under or came in contact with occasionally.

Certainly, the yearly talk given by Father Keating is superb. But the teachings of each of these folks would come home with me to be thoroughly discussed with Bob. We would find someone new such as Bernadette Roberts and get what we could from her and move on.

We would disagree but only in part with respect to some such as to John of the Cross. I would find him so moving I did not have to intellectualize him, but then Bob would admire Meister Eckert, and I could not completely understand him.

Throughout, there were many authors both Eastern and Western who I would look to him for explanation and sometimes not completely understand.

We would both enjoy the new writers like Diarmuid O'Murchu although he would usually think they did not go far enough.

Bob was brought up in a Roman Catholic home and at one time entered a seminary and another monastery. In neither did he stay very long. In his early adulthood, he examined the teachings of the Catholic Church and found them wanting.

He sees Jesus as a composite, questions most of the events that comprise Christian teachings, and has a negative attitude toward the fact that the teachings he learned growing up were false.

I never had figured out what I had believed growing up. I had it in my head that the teachings of Christ were authentic and they always did and I think always will serve me as a guide for the conduct of my life. With respect to the historical accuracy of the Christ story, it is nothing that worries me. I know enough not to take the bible literally, but I think if the Bible is the inspired word of God. I can go along with that because what I learned of the Christian teachings was an inspired body of learning so I just thank God for the inspiration and get on with it. There is no way I can express my appreciation and gratitude for having Bob in my life. We went together to hear the Taize given by Father Lizzotti in the beautiful chapel at Mount Carmel, we went to hear every speaker of what- ever religious persuasion from Matthew Fox to several rabbis.

We took a course together at U.B. in the Kaballah. We were both shocked that the Jewish community would permit such a limited rabbi to teach at a university level. It gave us occasion to get some knowledge of the Kaballah, but that was mainly from our own preparation to take the course. I spent considerable time with the Sufis at a time when Bob was not available, but whatever I studied, he would obtain the book and read it so we could discuss it. When we had the pleasure of Pier Valet coming to Buffalo it was but one more thrill. The Dalai Lama was at Cornell and it was an inspiration to meet him although he was not easy to understand.

Bob and I talk on the telephone and we still discuss our current thinking. He is teaching philosophy at a college in Florida and I think that presents a wonderful opportunity for the students.

In the meantime, I think of the many simple joys I have had in this quest: watching Thích run with the children on the grounds of Omega and all fall down, Barbara Walters rub noses with the Dalai Lama, the beauties of all the chants Gregorian, and other- wise.

One moment that summed it up was when Mary Ann, who did not have a jealous bone in her body, said to me, "Mary, I envy you, your spirituality."

It is freely given to anyone, and I know how fortunate I have been to not only make it such an all-consuming part of my life, but to also have a soul-mate companion on the journey who challenges my thinking.

I always felt in the work that I did that my all-consuming effort was to do what was right, to mete out justice, and to alleviate suffering. That has to be my only claim and my hope is that the result is that there were some lives that were made easier.

I spent about 25 years attending Mass at the Newman Center and was so inspired by the wonderful homilies delivered by Monsignor Weimer. To me, his last Mass (at least the one I attended) said it all when he expressed his hope that for the years, he preached the result would be that we would be a little nicer to one another. What a noble ambition!

Chapter Fifteen ω Conclusion

*"For always know
that we live by the love
we may never see."*

It is hard for me to collect my thoughts, which constitute the results of my spiritual endeavor, but surely, I can describe writers whose thinking I treasure:

The first is Yehudi Menuhin:

*"Human beings, as they are constituted,
seem to require a middleman, a broker,
between them and that great mystery
"the spirit within our hearts and
the way that is the truth."*

No one fulfills that role better than Jesus, the Jew, and the innocent man of truth who died in Jerusalem at the hands of his own people. (How many millions of innocents are being destroyed for and by the sins of all mankind?) Certainly, the crucified Jesus is sadly an apt symbol for the senseless cruelties of our world. Jesus, the living instrument of forgiveness, Buddha, a mirror to the inscrutable wisdom of mystic union with the Infinite: yet both app- roach each other, meet and overlap in their vows of poverty, in their "true wisdom, renunciation, and compassion."

What a comfort to have these symbols. What it stands for may differ from individual to individual or group to group, but it all stands for a beautiful cosmic reality that humanity reached such a height. My chosen way of prayer has always been through meditation, which Yehudi Menuhin describes as "to share a secret with God, without understanding the secret, yet enjoying a living communion with the greater unknowable."

"The methodology for this activity is described by William James in a manner very meaningful to me.

'Mystical facilities' here refers to that flood-tide of inner warmth and vital energy that human beings regard as the most vital state to live in. Pure presence, uncontaminated clarity, like that of a mirror that reflects everything, which is man's true treasure.

Concentration of energies is undoubtedly one of the most important conditions of the state the saint's call 'Innikeit' inwardness. The saint achieves inwardness by a deliberate policing of the vital energies. He comes to recognize the energy- stealing emotion, all the emotions that do not make for inwardness and he sets out to exterminate them in himself. As he moves toward his objective, he increases steadily his supply of surplus vital power, and so increases his powers of foresight and hind- sight, the sense of other times and other places; there is a breaking free of the body's sense of imprisonment in time and a rising warmth of life energy that is spoken of in the Gospel as 'to have life more abundantly.'

This seems to me what one might call a Western approach, but I also find the Eastern writers, while more difficult to understand, to represent Truth.

Nomakkai Morbu has said, "Dzogchen doesn't ask you to change your religion, philosophy, or ideology, nor to become something other than what you are. It only asks you to observe yourself and to discover the 'cage' you have built with all your conditioning and limits, and it teaches you how to get out of the cage without creating another one in order to become a free, autonomous person." In fact, Dzogchen teaches how to regain that freedom of being which we all potentially have.

Freedom, in this case, means a state in which one is no longer conditioned by dualism, by judgments, by the passions, and by everything, one believes in. One might ask, "But what then is left of a person?" The method used by Norbu is that of a continuous presence of awareness.

Harvard Professor William James, one of the most insightful and stimulating of American philosophers, defined religion as:

*"The belief that there is an unseen order
and that our supreme good
lies in harmonically adjusting ourselves thereto."*

I would be remiss if I did not include Bob's letter to me in response to my lack of clarity with respect to Albert Low's methodology.

September 17th, 2006

Mary,

*In regard to Albert Low, he is teaching a method known as the Five Ranks, the Go-1, which I will outline below:
The purpose of all eastern meditation is to deconstruct the inner dialogue, the cycle of subject and object, which creates the world as we know it. In order to achieve this, the automatic responses we give to percepts must cease. This is how mindfulness is sup- posed to be taught. It is not the suppression of thought or identification with any object. It is the lack of response, which will eventually lead to a cessation of the cycle itself.*

In due time, awareness will shift from the psyche to the body itself. When this occurs, awareness will tend to continue even during sleep. Finally, there is a cessation of all mental activities. If attention is maintained even during this period called Nirodha, awareness breaks loose entirely from the body and mind. When this state of one's identity of the surroundings and the self is perm- anent, one is said to have reached enlightenment.

*Low's method is to reset in two positions—Host and Guest. He calls them self-as-center and self-as-periphery. The Host is the usual subjective position—self-awareness. The Guest is the object
—objects of attention—percepts. One moves back and forth be- tween the subjective and objective positions until any distinction between them ends. At this point, awareness moves, as above, into the body and eventually is detached even from that in samadhi trance. Coming out of this state then leads to the breakthrough.*

Love Bob

Epilogue

*You can search the world over
and you will find no one
who is more deserving of
   your kindness
   and well wishing
than yourself.*
                        —Buddha

Christianity, as described by Yehudi Menuhin, resonates in my soul. To me, Buddhism is a beautiful, serene philosophy to partake of which has given me untold pleasure.

We have examples of humans who have achieved trans- forming experiences, Thomas Aquinas, a Doctor of the Church "saw the curtain move" and said throw away all of my voluminous theological sayings and writings. They did not mean anything.

I believe Thomas Merton was given a glimpse at 22nd and Walnut after many years as a hermit.
Buddha became enlightened as he sat under the Bodhi Tree. I mention them individually because it is my belief that very few human beings attain this spiritual development.

And what is this? Our language does not have words to describe it. All we really know is that each of us has some thirst to want "to know." And, I submit to reach this experience it would have to be in silence.

I feel very gifted to be aware of the joy that can flow from the practice as well as the companionship of the many sincere people who are also on the journey.

As one of the astronauts said, "This is such a beautiful blue globe that it seems impossible that we don't all treasure it." The lesson is as simple as that, love could solve humanity's problems. I have reached an age where I am unqualifiedly thankful for having experienced the elements of life as described by Yehudi Menuhin, that is, that sense of infinity, of tragedy, of joy, of struggle and of dream. I have not accomplished the ability to see with my ears or hear with my eyes, but there each is still extant and the hope that one day I will be that child who enters the Kingdom.

"It is the thinking of the mystic that humans must move be- yond the superficial prayer of words to have the direct experience of encountering The Other, which is accomplished through silence. A most meaningful description of this experience is one"

by Pierre Teilhard de Chardin:

I took the lamp and, leaving the zone of everyday occupation and relationships where everything seems clear, I went down into my innermost self, to the deep abyss whence I feel dimly that my power of action emanates, but as I moved further and further away from the conventional certainties by which social life is superficially illuminated, I became aware that I
was losing contact with myself.

At each step of the descent a new person was disclosed within me of whose name I was no longer sure, and who no longer obeyed me, and when I had to stop my exploration because the path faded beneath my steps, I found a bottomless abyss at my feet, and out of it came—arising I know not from where—the current which I dare to call my life.

I think to believe in the mystical without having the actual experience required a strong intuitive belief. This belief, without the experience, is sustainable through the other fruits, which flow naturally from the silent meditative practice.

Appendix I Diagnostic Study of a Personality

A—— is a man in his early seventies. He is medium height, average weight, moderately well-dressed, with a pleasant to "good looking" face. He is courteous, reserved, or shy it is hard to know which adjective to use, and if one looks very closely at him, it is possible to perceive that he has some sort of eye defect.

Historically
A—— is of Irish-English ancestry with his immediate family religious background Catholic and his immediate family political background Democratic. He is not the product of a mixed marriage but his paternal grandfather was born in England and Protestant. The rest of his heritage as far as known is Irish and Catholic.

A——'s father was a tradesman, painter and worked seasonally but the family was moderately well off as a result of thrifty planning. A——'s mother was a housewife who had six children and devoted herself exclusively to her children and her church. Her devout religious interest was shared by her husband. She had no other community interests and verbalized a relative disinterest in her husband, referring to him as "alright, he's a good man."
A——'s father often referred to his wife as a "wooden woman."

Biologically
A—— was the second child born in his family. His mother had an "easy" pregnancy and a normal delivery. A——'s father was a diabetic who died in his early middle age from this disease. A——'s mother was in "good" health up to the time of her death in her late eighties from an accidental fall. A—— did not have any of the extreme childhood diseases and has only known illness in the form of high blood pressure during the 1930s. The only time A—— has been a patient in a hospital was as a result of being pounded in the face by a "hold-up" man which resulted in a loss of vision in one eye, a loosening of teeth, and a compound fracture of the hand

A—— is completely amnesic concerning this occurrence, the only amnesia he has suffered in his life, but which made it impossible for him to identify his assailant. This incident happened when A—— was in his early sixties, but his hand is completely recovered and stomach trouble, which occurred after the accident, disappeared, with the removal of teeth.

Childhood
A—— did better than average in school, getting marks in the eighties, but was considered the least bright in his family. He quit school after graduating from 9th grade, although his father admonished him that he would regret it and would not be allowed to return to school. He was a nice-looking child who was well-liked by other children and adults and early established a reputation for unusual veracity. He was never considered a behavior problem although he indulged in the usual childhood "pranks" but did have a reputation for being "scrappy," physically and verbally if what he considered his rights were threatened. He was extremely religious and chauvinistic in regard to his Irish ancestry.

Adolescence
A—— started to work at about 13 as a machinist's helper and various other early-adult semi-skilled occupations. He soon decided he had made a mistake in not getting an education and tried to attend night school. This he found almost impossibly laborious after walking to and from work at which he spent twelve hours a day. He did, however, attempt to "improve" his mind through reading, mainly in history, but fact, rarely fiction.

A—— was not the typical American boy. During this period A—— decided to try to save his money for passage to Ireland where he would dedicate himself to the "cause" of helping to free the enslaved people from the English.
Before he got underway on this venture he was influenced by people and reading both, that the situation was being gotten under control and further that this type of situation had a dual nature rather than "bad guys" and "good guys." A change took place in

A——'s personality during these years. He was brought almost completely under the influence of those believing in pure reason. That emotions are not to be displayed but rather situations, attacks, problems, should be given thought, consideration, and be acted on verbally.

Very rarely after A——'s youth did he overtly lose his temper but rather used the method of absorbing, i.e., insults, and waiting patiently to give his unsuspecting opponent a verbal blow.

A——'s childhood scrappiness was buried, he now had the reputation of being very good natured and easy to get along with. A—— decided he would see something of the world outside his home city and traveled down the east coast of the US picking up jobs as a machinist in various towns and cities. Then the economic panic of the early 1900s hit the USA, and much to his amazement could no longer pick up jobs with ease. He returned to his home city where he was sure he could find work but instead soon found he was evading his friends because of the shame of not having a job.

He then wondered what caused this and spent his time in the library reading on the subject of economics. He took to an anti-capitalistic philosophy immediately and so he found a "cause" on which he could keep mentally busy for the rest of his life.

A—— became very active in the labor movement, going from plant to plant to organize and convention after convention to rally. He always took the same position with the men, i.e., never let them see your feelings but wait until the time is right and then strike quickly and quietly. The violence, at this time, he abhorred but mainly saw it as a result of management practices.
He argued violently with his associates in the labor movement regarding the Catholic Church. When a specific occasion arose, the Child Labor Amendment, A—— had no sympathy for the con position of the Church and went to the local college for an apology. No explanation given satisfied

him and he started to question the whole of the teachings of the Church. A—— changed from a daily communicant to attending church on Sunday through habit, family and neighborhood pressures, while at the same time "knocking" everything it stood for to anyone who would listen, and particularly to devout Catholics.

A—— spent his time, socially, mainly in the company of men, drinking beer evenings at a men's club connected with the church. He had several close relationships, which were to last his whole life, some among ultra-conservatives; some among violent radicals but he was forever the enemy of the Irish politician of which there were many in his club.

He took girls out to about the extent necessary for i.e. dances always conscious that they shouldn't get the wrong idea about his serious intentions, never "taking advantage" of them, and inevitably "sizing them up" with the premise that "it would be better to marry a prostitute than a selfish woman."

There was one woman that he went with sporadically starting in his early twenties and continuing for about twelve years. He considered her an intelligent, capable woman but in the final analysis, she had too much of a temper to make a good wife. He would also casually mention that she was an APA Protestant and his mother would probably never be able to believe that he would marry outside of the Church.
Later Early Adult
A—— decided that he really should get a socialistic job to beat the business cycle and so he took the exam for the Railway Mail. At about the same time the labor organization, of which he was a member, suggested that some members should open stores carrying exclusively union made goods. A—— opened the first store of this type in the locality, part of the financing coming from money borrowed from his mother.

Shortly after A—— went into business he received an appointment on the railway Mail, which after much debate he refused. His business was a moderately successful one at first although he early found this was not the result of patronage from Union members, friends or family but rather location, good service, word of mouth, etc. He felt this was just a fact of life so nobody should be bitter about it. During this period, A—— devoted a lot of his time to the study of history and economics while at his place of business, rather than keeping the shelves in order, and still spent most of his free time attending union meetings and drinking beer with men at his club. It was also during this period that he met a girl at the beach who was one of a group of school teachers and took her dancing a few times over a period of two summers.

Courtship and Marriage
A—— knew his wife for 4 to 5 years prior to marriage but the actual courtship was between two and three years.
A—— started off very cautiously with his wife seeing her rarely until he could "size her up" and finally getting to the stage where he saw her regularly and would feel free to accept an invitation to her home. The next step was introducing her to his mother and when she reached the threshold of his mother's living room, he tripped her so her first introduction to his family necessitated her getting up off the floor.

A—— states that he voluntarily gave his wife an engagement ring but it always appears that there might have been some subtle 'undue influence on her part. A—— then found himself subjected to severe pressure from his fiancée to set a date for the wedding. He explained to her over and over that there was a recession, that he was losing money, and that the whole capitalist system was doomed in the near future. A——'s fiancée still wanted the date. A—— and his mother got together and bought two two-family adjoining houses with plans for A——'s mother to live down in one and A, with his wife, to live down in the other. A—— was married shortly thereafter at the age of 36.

The mother of A——'s wife's died when she was two. She had seven brothers. Her father found it necessary to board her, and her sister, in a convent and hire a housekeeper to maintain a home for him and his sons. A——'s father-in- law was very comfortable financially. A——'s wife and sister were taken a few years later by five maternal maiden aunts and raised by them.

A——'s wife attended convent schools through high school and then "the Teacher's College. She was raised in a home where there was a great emphasis on the intellectual and artistic values and sufficient money to travel and entertain extensively. Her Aunts were extremely conservative in their views. A——'s wife became somewhat anti-intellectual as a result of the fact that her Aunts were given to a great deal of private quarreling and she was inclined to wonder what all their "corresponding in French" accomplished when they could achieve no daily piece of mind. A——'s wife was carefully protected from men but was determined to marry although, even at age 27, when she did marry there were grave threats that all of her Aunts might go into a decline over the situation!

A——'s Career
Relatively early things took a turn for the worse in A——'s business and recoveries did not reach the peak of declines. During the thirties A—— operated mainly on a past reputation for integrity and postdated checks. A——'s place of business was as much a gathering place for working men "free thinkers" as it was a place for economic gain.

A—— never acknowledged any personal responsibility for problems connected with i.e. the inability to buy new shoes when the others became too small for his children because everyone was existing under a faulty economy. With the early forties A—— was no longer steadily losing capital (although he never thereafter rose above the low- income bracket), but there were some inheritances from his and his wife's family and his wife returned to teaching so while he continued to speak in gloomy terms concerning the next depression and conducting himself as though the '30s were still extant, he actually had no financial problem.

When A——'s son graduated from college as a physics major and with a fellowship for graduate work A—— pointed out once that a young fellow might really be able to make something of his business, but when his son became upset by the suggestion, he dropped it quickly.

A——'s Marriage

A—— considers himself thrice blessed to have had a happy marriage for over 35 years and feels that it is conclusive proof that it was worthwhile for him to be forbearing and tolerant of all his wife's faults down through the years. It is a slight disappointment to A—— that he has never been able to convince his wife of the fallacy of the Catholic Church, the capitalist system, or being interested in having a little extra money for a bottle of gin but one of his favorite phrases is "Nowhere is a prophet without honor save in his own country." His marriage has been punctuated with various relatives, starting with his mother, living with him and his wife and three children. This left a minimum of time for him and his wife to spend together, so his married life at home consisted almost entirely of reading with rare Sunday drives.

His unfortunate accident above described left him unable to do any prolonged reading in his early sixties. This was at a time when all the "live-in" relatives were dead and his three children had left or were about to leave home. During their early married years, practically all bitter arguments were concerning finances but they no longer have any reasonable possibility of a financial problem, and A—— spends a great deal of time keeping himself physically and mentally fit and trying to convince his wife to do so. He has finally relinquished his lifelong interest in political economics, to some extent, in favor of food faddism and health projects. He and his wife work together and have many friends with whom they have pleasant sociable times and A—— states that if heaven is anything like this he will be satisfied, with an obvious conclusive presumption that that is where he is going.

Appendix II ◊Sri Lanka

We drink from wells we did not dig; we are warmed by fires we did not build.

—paraphrased from Deuteronomy 6:11

We left the ship by mini-bus. I always get anxiety-ridden for fear I won't find my way and everyone else walks too fast for me. Then I get slightly paranoid about it. We were approached by a deluge of cab drivers, but no beggars initially and in fact, very little during our whole stay in Sri Lanka. There was one man without arms and several children with hands out. (Note: The nun we were with said that she did not want to take too much because the villagers were poor and did not have much to eat. More on this later.) It was very pleasant stopping for fruit along the way. Driving through Columbo seemed similar to Bombay in terms of being commercial, but there were not people lying all over the street and the stores were not nearly as makeshift looking.

A hotel left over from the British was pointed out and I resolved to return to it.

(We did and it was as charming as it was luxurious, similar to the King Eddie, Claridge's, etc. It was called the Galle Face and it was originally built in 1864. We had a gin and tonic and looked over the Indian Ocean). As we continued our drive to the Nun's Island, we passed lovely homes some with gingerbread architecture. Also, hotels that looked beautiful. (We stopped at one on the way back—very tropical—all marble and columns, one room flowing into the other. The sunset at the Indian Ocean was lovely. The trip took longer than we expected and we arrived after dark to be greeted by Mister De Silva at the Rest House. (De Silva is a common name, Portuguese origin and Rest House is synonymous with Guest House.)

There were seventeen of us and on arrival Mr. De Silva expressed dismay at only having three bedrooms. Our tour leader said we had all been informed of this fact and it was completely acceptable.

We were offered a glass of papaya juice but I am very careful of my stomach and drank coke (I would have preferred a gin and tonic.). We shared a bedroom with the only other married couple. It had two double beds covered by mosquito netting. When we arrived, Judith, (who is a Buddhist) went into the bathroom and was attacked by a lizard. She screamed and her husband came to her rescue by removing the lizard from her. (She was a Buddhist, so she did not want to harm any living creature.) It inhibited my bladder sufficiently that I slept through the night without using the bathroom.

Dinner consisted of all kinds of Indian oddities, many of which were very hot and I enjoyed it very much. Bill ate little since his stomach is "off" some. (My health has been a miracle the whole trip and I have even lost a few pounds). After dinner, we had a visit by the head sister from the Island.

The location of the guesthouse appears at night to be dead center in a tropical forest with just a path leading to it. It is on a lake with the moon shining on it and the water lapping against the canoes hoisted on the dock. (There are all kinds of tropical birds and sounds like fireflies.)

Out of the night walked a young woman named Philippa who was from England but dressed in the Indian costume from the Punjab, which is loose-fitting trousers with an over-dress.

She had come to spend three months in meditation with the nuns. She is 26 years old and had been trekking for approximately one month alone in India—she said she had had no trouble and felt safe. I asked her if she minded having her head shaved. She replied that she was not overly attached to her hair. Mister De Silva told her she would have to sleep on the floor. (The students who had to sleep on the floor told me they were being eaten alive so they told the others sleeping lengthwise in double beds to pull their feet up and they crawled under the matting and slept horizontally.)

Sister visited with us from 9:30 to approximately 10:30. She came with an entourage consisting of a boatman, a woman attendant—I think one of the other nuns and some other man whose function I did not determine.

Her purpose was to welcome us and talk with some generality about the method of transportation to the island, arrangements for lunch, pads for us to sit on, etc. She talked to Judith about the nun's movement and its relationship to the power structure and the dharma (truths) of Theravada Buddhism. She also acknowledged the planned arrival of Phillippa. After she paddled away there was some desultory conversation and everyone went their way for the night with notice that breakfast was at 6:00 AM.

Again, I wished I had a Manhattan before sleep but since we can't use the ice in these countries there was no sense in bringing anything so we went straight to bed. The bed was high and quite hard and there was no cover of any kind, not even a sheet. During the night, the fan created a draft that made our feet cold but we just suffered through it.

In the morning, we showered with no soap or could not brush our teeth. Breakfast consisted of papaya which was delicious and all sorts of food like fried eggs in a thin crepe. I ate little! Bill ate his egg. We then assembled to paddle over to the nuns. I was scared I was so fat that I would capsize the boat. There were five of us to a boat (seven in the canoe) and one boat-man with one paddle for the half-hour ride. He weighed about 130 pounds—*if that*.

When we arrived, we went to the meditation hall where we sat on mats. I am just not constructed for cross-legged sitting so I was not comfortable. The sisters assembled ahead of us. There was approximately a dozen. The head nun from Australia (origin- ally German), two other German nuns, two from Sweden, two from Britain, two from America.

Ordaining a woman, a Buddhist nun in Sri Lanka is for- bidden so Sister was ordained in Hong Kong. She spoke of some trouble with the establishment in the initiating of the nunnery, that they would be unprotected therefore all robbed and raped and anyway they were anathema. However, she said it was all talk and they had a fine relationship with the villagers and the monks who were on a nearby little island.

She talked a little of Theravada Buddhism and made it sound simple and appealing. She described their life of once a week taking their begging bowls to one of the four neighboring villages and that the villagers treated it as a festival day and also were honored to give. She said they could come back with truck-loads but they didn't want to take too much as the people could not spare that much. We did twenty minutes of meditation and I either had some reaction or the heat got to me.

The sisters then led tours of the island. I did not go since it was extremely hot but sat on the porch with Virginia who is from Jamaica. She attends Stanford and is, I imagine, from a wealthy family, since there are only very rich and poor among Jamaicans.

Sister came along and we spoke of the beauty of the island, she remarked that there was no reason for poverty such as India's since the palm tree can provide, food, shelter, and clothing. I asked her if idle chatter was forbidden. She said it was except as was necessary for the functioning of life.

In the morning, she had described how she spent her time. She apparently has a large correspondence through the world, reads current germane writings, and preaches one dharma with a single interpreter (who is one of the nuns and can translate al-most simultaneously). Visitors do chores with the nuns at times. They must eat their one meal a day before noon and obviously would not share (except with Phillipa since they begged for the food). They usually have a cook from the village. (I am writing this on deck and continuously interrupted.) Sister is much taller sitting down than standing up. I remarked on this. She is a very poised woman and answered that many people are surprised at how little there is of her.

After lunch, she gave another little talk, did a meditation where she led us through a thinking process of reaching out to those with whom we are associated and encompassing our enemies with love. (I asked Bill if he thought it appropriate to send a postcard to Peter Mullany signed Love Mary Davey—he laughed—maybe it's not funny).

After a blessing, the nuns all put up their parasols and walked in their bare feet to the back of the deck to bid us farewell and we paddled off to the Guest House where we had an Indian Lunch. I did not eat much.

On the trip home, we lost most of the students—some got off to climb Adams Peak (a mountain) where they could watch the sunrise for Easter morning the next day, others to motorcycle around the island and still others to check into a hotel and go snorkeling.

We stopped the minibus to buy a bottle of gin. Had a good strong martini, a little dinner and collapsed.

Appendix III ◊ Lichtenstein Letters

January 9th, 1979 (handwritten)
Dear Ms. Davey:
Thank you for letting me knows about your father's death. There is not much that words can do to alleviate the sense of bereavement and loss. I want to let you know, however, that I feel great sympathy for you for having suffered this loss during a period of estrangement. It is very clear to me that there has been a lifelong striving on your part to win your father's recognition as a person who has always aimed at achievements that would please your father—and make him proud of you. I often suspected that he might, in fact, have been aware of what you have accomplished, but was unable to express the admiration that he may have felt. He seems to have had great difficulties to express affection. He was apparently a man who was very proud to have done what he wanted, and I think you inherited some of this determination. I hope you will continue in that direction in honor of your father.

Cordially,
Heinz Lichtenstein

910 Kings Mill Road
Chapel Hill, N.C. 27514
Telephone 919-967-7964

February 4, 1980
Dear Ms. Davey:
Thank you very much for your letter of December 26, 1979, and for your good wishes for the New Year, which I reciprocate sincerely.

Reading your letter made me very aware of the intense external and internal pressures that complicate your life so very much, and that makes you inclined to seek some form of instant relief when you perceive the tensions as intolerable.

What is equally impressive to me is the fact that in spite of these difficulties you are capable to live up to the demands of a very strenuous and responsible career, and are also responsive to the stimulations of life that you.

You are able to enjoy travel, change of scenery, art in many forms, especially literature and theater. All this proves that in spite of the many and painful frustrations that you are suffering, you have never really withdrawn from life, but are always open to it and can derive genuine satisfaction from participating in it to the fullest. I think that is a very encouraging fact of your existence because the frustrations and disappointments of life can lead to an emotional withdrawal that makes some persons truly isolated and incapable to respond to anything that life may offer to them. It does not take any intense prodding for you to reach out for whatever opportunity of participating in a full life you may encounter, you are particularly responsive to human interaction, perhaps your need for such interaction is a real base for whatever addictions you struggle with. Your tendency to drink too much or to overeat are probably ways to satisfy the yearning for human closeness whenever that need is frustrated. This yearning is so intense that it makes me feel that one of the underlying un- resolved problems, in the language of modern child analysts, is the difficulty of separation (of the infant from the mother) which is the prerequisite for the process of individuation. From what I know about your upbringing, I would not at all be surprised if such circumstances actually did exist. It sometimes leads in children to an overemphasis on premature and excessive independence as a means to overcome the need for being mothered. Such situations are always leading to difficult problems in adult life. Nevertheless, your responsiveness to human interaction present in the critical early phase of your life, because one does not long for something that one has never known. You are doing as well as you do—in spite of inner difficulties— because whatever your early frustrations might have been, they never deprived you of hope for emotional resonance from somebody whom you perceived as a caring adult.

Thus, even though I am aware of your tensions and frustrations, I am always confident of the power of some latent strength in you that will not fail you in the long struggle for a harmonious life.

Sincerely,
Heinz Lichtenstein

May 16, 1981

Dear Ms. Davey:

Your telephone call was a surprise when it came, and the news of your marriage made it, in spite of all conflicts concerning this decision, a distinctly pleasant surprise; it seems to be a sign of important developments in your growth as a person.

Your letter, which I received yesterday, confirms that impression. Your anxieties and uncertainties seem to me due to your aware- ness of a clash of irreconcilable* definitions of yourself as a person: there is a striving forward as a person: there is a striving toward total independence that is incompatible with powerful dependency needs; a power but need for self-assertion and equality in a "masculine' world, but equally strong needs for recognition of your feminine potentialities which make your yearning for a person who would be understanding of your needs to be taken care of and be protective toward you. I do have the impression that you perceive Bill as an individual who understands these seemingly incompatible needs in you, respects them, and does not insist on your making a choice between them. I hope this sensitivity on his part will create a setting in which you can live "in harmony not only with him but also with yourself. I believe that you are aware that Bill possibly has conflicts similar to those that you have struggled with, and he might never have had a partner who had this insight. I hope very sincerely that you will find in each other a way of understanding that will contribute to a better life for both of you. With my warm good wishes,
     Sincerely,
     Heinz Lichtenstein

Bibliography

1: The Psychoanalytic Study of the Child, 1946 - Phyllis Green- acre M.D. | "birth— leaves unique and individual traces that are superimposed on the genetically determined anxiety and libidinal patterns of the given infant"

2: Emotional Maturity: The Development and Dynamics of Personality, 1949 - Leon J Saul | "unassimilated superego— no- thing intrinsically wrong with mother's standards but he was never won over to accepting them as part of himself and integrating them into his personality—. He developed high blood pressure."

3: Stress and Disease, 1914 - Harold G. Wolff | "In our society the protective symptoms mentioned are commonly found in essentially passive non- participating persons who have been made angry by situations that they cannot or do not face."

4: Emotional Maturity: The Development and Dynamics of Personality, 1949 - Leon J Saul | "Conspicuously close to mother—put all emotional eggs in one basket—under severe emotional stress developed amnesic fugues."

5: American Catholic Family, 1957 - Rev John L Thomas | "The Catholic immigrant groups faced the problem of establishing themselves in a society which had been pre-empted by Anglo- Saxon Protestantism. This put the Catholic families on the defensive and intensified their minority status."

6: Growing Up in New Guinea, 1930 - Margaret Mead | "The American boy's conceptions of manhood are diluted, standardized, undifferentiated. His choices are as generic as his vision. He chooses to make money, to be a success, he makes no particularistic allegiances."

7: Social Casework: A Problem-Solving Process, 1957 - Helen Harris Perlman | "A person at any stage of his life not only is a "product" of nature and nurture but is also and always "in process" of being in the present and becoming in the future."

8: On Being Human, 1950 - Ashley Montagu | "Kropotkin attempt- ed to show that there is an unconscious force throughout the realm of living nature which is expressed as an unconscious mutualism which serves to produce greater survival value for every form of life—"

9: American Catholic Family, 1957 - Rev John L Thomas | "In occupational status, the Irish showed a tendency to higher per- centages in the "while collar" classes."

10: Pub. unknown, Author unknown | "The Irish—in regard to length of acquaintance and engagement, there was a marked tendency for marriage after a relatively long acquaintance and engagement period—age at marriage more advanced than average."

11: Pub. Social Work Journal, Author unknown | "Again, it may be that marginal existence with freedom will be infinitely preferable to comfort and plenty under the rule of enforced authority."

12: What Strong Family Life Means in Our Society, 1953 - Kimball Young | "An external element that influences family life is the business cycle—wife may become chief wage earner—reduction of husband's status may prove to be severe blow to ego."

ABOUT THE AUTHOR

Mary K. Davey-Carr was the first female appointed Administrative Law Judge for the State of New York and achieved national recognition when she received an award for her outstanding decision writing. A native of Buffalo, she attended the University at Buffalo School of Law, was a charter member of the Law Review and became a graduate of the class of 1952. Her exceptional law career was as varied as it was demanding.

Prior to retirement, she married William Carr and traveled extensively around the world, including Australia and Africa. Her remarkable journey developed into a major interest in spirituality, which she still pursues today.

Made in the USA
Lexington, KY
19 September 2019